Contents

Acknowledgments

I remember once hearing Lucy Calkins describe her work as "standing on the shoulders" of researchers who came before her. I know what she means. This book represents the thinking of many. I am grateful to the teachers at Roberts Avenue School in Danbury, Connecticut, for the wise work they do every day and for allowing me to work alongside them. Much of the thinking in this book grew out of our work together. Thank you especially to Marie Langdon, Anna Rocco, Chris Pruss, Jan Edwards, Yolanda Longoria, Kathy Hamilton, Michele Masi, and Kay Kopec.

Thank you also to the teachers in Connecticut's District 6, who are under the wise direction of Denise Bozutto. This book is filled with the echoes of conversations with you, as well as with teachers at Stillmeadow School, Tracey School, and Hayestown School in Connecticut, and Mannetuck, Bellew, and Captree Schools in West Islip, New York. Thank you to the teachers at Parkway School, Springhurst School, and Scotland School for letting me take photos of your rooms.

Thank you to Lucy Calkins, Isoke Nia, and the staff at the Teachers College Reading and Writing Project for continually stretching my thinking.

Thank you to my colleague, Lynn Holcomb. How important it has been to know that I can bounce ideas off you anytime day or night! Thank you mostly for your friendship.

Thank you to Wendy Murray and Raymond Coutu from Scholastic for your patience and wise guidance in editing this book. You made the process such a grand adventure!

Thank you Mimi, PopPop, Tony, and Kirstin for picking up the slack. I appreciate everything you do more than you'll know. It's such a comfort to know that my kids don't "skip a beat" when I am working.

Emily and Robert, you teach me something new every day. Thank you for bringing to life all of my beliefs about learning and teaching.

To my husband and best friend, Rob, thank you. How much it means to know that I can count on you always!

Introduction

Balancing the Needs to Plan Our Teaching and to Continually Revise Our Ideas

"Time spent planning and thinking about how we want our teaching to go is never wasted time. It is the most worthwhile investment in excellent teaching we can make."
—Katie Wood Ray

*O*ver the years in my work as a staff developer, I have had the opportunity—the privilege, really—to work alongside a countless number of teachers from a variety of different classrooms. I've worked in urban and suburban settings, with large school districts and small ones, in schools where sixty percent of the population speaks a language other than English, and so on.

I've been able to see for myself how the latest research in literacy teaching is being translated in the real world. I've often thought how valuable those experiences and insights would be if I were still teaching in the classroom full time. Teaching can be such an isolating career. Some of us are fortunate enough to be working in a community that fosters collegiality and risk taking. Most of us are not, however. We close our doors and do what we do, alone.

The recent political fervor over accountability is scary. Society's ills are being blamed on schools. Policy makers are making rash decisions based on knee-jerk reactions to public sentiment, which is being fed by the media. I've worked with teachers who have told me, "I want to include more independent reading and writing in my program, but you don't understand—my test scores were the lowest . . ." And, "They keep adding more to my curriculum. Now I have to teach the character program. I just don't have the time to let the kids read and write." Where are our priorities?

I worked with a group of principals recently. We were taking a look at current best practices and considering how they, as educational leaders, could support the work in their schools. After listening to me describe what should be happening in primary literacy classrooms, one principal said, "I don't care how the teacher does it, just as long as she gets the job done." He didn't feel it was necessary to ask some teachers to change what they had been doing for the past twenty years, as long as they were getting high test scores. A comprehensive literacy program starts with a much broader definition of "getting the job done." Good test scores are important, especially in the politically charged arena that education has become. But how sad if that is our only measure of success in literacy teaching.

Literacy "giants" (Marie Clay, Donald Graves, Ken Goodman, Lucy Calkins, Katie Wood Ray, Sharon Taberski, and Gay Su Pinnell, to name just a few) have spent years informing our teaching. What I respect most about these educators is that they are constantly refining their work based on what they see happening in classrooms. This can be overwhelming and even frustrating for those of us who don't like it when things are "always changing." But, I've come to realize that change is good. Research is constantly providing us with new information. We need to stay up to date in order to provide the best instruction to our students. As long as we keep the goal of teaching the readers and writers in our classrooms, as opposed to teaching a program or a textbook, we'll continue to grow.

As a new teacher, so much of my energy was spent focusing on what I, the teacher, was doing. I read the teacher's manuals to tell me what to say and how to say it. I decided on what to teach based on the curriculum guidelines. Over time, though, I began attending summer institutes at the Reading and Writing Project at Teachers College. I began to read professional books on literacy learning. And my teaching changed.

I began to focus on the children, the learners. I learned to use running records which informed my teaching. I paid attention to the students' needs and interests which also informed my teaching. The bulletin boards in the room became more interactive. The students organized the class library. I added a writing workshop and a reading workshop.

But, despite all those changes, I had a nagging feeling that I wasn't "getting to it all." So there is more balance in what I do now. I still focus on the children, but within a framework of an understanding of good literacy teaching. That's why I wrote this book, to help you walk the fine line between carefully framing curriculum while being open to new tides of ideas and the tug from students who require something different from what you planned.

This book grew out of my professional life, which now focuses on helping teachers realize that they can make changes in their programs which will *develop* the readers and writers who do well on standardized tests because they can read and write well. Although the work feels different in every school, with every group of children and with every teacher, there are basic truths, a vision if you will, that remains the same. This book is for teachers who believe that:

* all students can learn to read and write.
* students need to be *taught* strategies for reading and writing, and not just be given reading and writing assignments.
* there is a developmental continuum for learning to read and write, and teachers need to be able to assess students to determine where they fall on that continuum.
* authentic assessment should drive instruction.
* the best teachers are *researchers of teaching and learning* who continually outgrow many of their own ideas.

The most effective teachers understand the difference between teaching readers/writers and assigning reading/writing. They have moved beyond merely covering the curriculum to focusing on the students. Districts spend a lot of time and money trying to find the "perfect program." There is no such thing. There are, however, accepted best practices which are supported by research.

🔖 What This Book Contains

In Part I, you'll learn why planning is important in a comprehensive, balanced literacy program. It is not my intention to tell you what to teach and how to teach it, but rather how to use the planning process to make the best of your methods. The idea of *intentional teaching* and how it best meets the true needs of our students while helping us feel in control is the focus of Chapter 1.

Each of us has a different knowledge base and comfort level with teaching reading and writing. It is helpful to have a common language so we can have a dialogue. We're all learning more about literacy teaching all the time as we try to bridge the gap between what is and what should be. So in Chapter 2, I take a brief look at current best practices in comprehensive, balanced literacy programs.

Chapter 3, "Beginning Your Curriculum Binders: Using Units of Study to Plan Your Reading and Writing Workshop," provides an overview and examples of typical units of study in literacy for K–2 classrooms.

If Part I of this book is about why to plan for the year in a comprehensive literacy program, Part II is about *how*. You will find step-by-step guidelines for planning your curriculum. Chapters 4, 5, and 6 describe how to begin with a year-long plan and translate that plan into monthly and, eventually, daily lessons. I offer some ideas for professional development, accompanying reproducible forms, and a bibliography at the end.

Throughout this book, I'll ask you to carry out short writing tasks to help you think about and assimilate new information. If you are using this book as part of a professional discussion group, your responses will help guide productive conversations. Take the time to respond thoughtfully while working through the process of planning.

Katie Wood Ray, in her book, *The Writing Workshop: Working Through the Hard Parts (And They're All Hard Parts)*, reminds us not to lose sight of why we need to plan and be articulate about our planning. Planning intentionally not only helps us explain ourselves better to others, but also informs our day-to-day teaching decisions because we'll be clear about what we are doing and why we are doing it. Katie's work and others' (including the work of Isoke Nia, Director of Research and

Development at The Reading and Writing Project, Teachers College) can give us the courage to stop asking for lists of 180 mini-lessons or a curriculum guide for workshop teaching and to start thinking for ourselves—to start asking, "What makes sense for me and the students in my classroom?"

Curriculum comes from a variety of places. Each state and district has its own mandates. There are new standards for literacy teaching all the time. Individual teachers have different expertise and interests. And then, of course, one has to consider the particular needs of the children in our classrooms. Over the years, I have been guiding teachers in creating curriculum plans for reading and writing workshops that balance all of these factors. My goal in writing this book is to help you be more intentional in your teaching and more purposeful in your planning as you work on putting it all together.

Part I
Why Plan?

The Power of Intentional Teaching

How Does Your Current Practice Measure Up?

teach—To teach someone is etymologically to "show" something. The word goes back to the prehistoric Indo-European base deik ("show"), which also produced Greek deiknunai "show" (source of English paradigm) and Latin dicere ("say") (source of English diction, dictionary, etc). Its Germanic descendant was taik-, which produced English token and German zeigen ("show"). From it was derived the verb taikjan, ancestor of English teach.
—Dictionary of Word Origins

*F*or our teaching to be powerful, we need to be intentional. We need to have a plan. In this chapter, we will take the initial steps to becoming intentional in our curriculum planning.

🔔 Naming Our Goals for Our Students

I begin by asking you to reflect on these bedrock questions:

What does it mean to write well?

What does it mean to read well?

Thinking about these questions will help you discover and define what you are after when teaching reading and writing. Your yearly, monthly, and daily plans, which we will focus on in later chapters, will all emanate from these core goals. Now take a few minutes to write down answers to the questions below.

The Qualities of Good Writers and Readers

Think about a "good" writer you know—a writer who is independent, mature, and strong. It may be yourself or another adult you know. What does it mean to write well? What does a good writer do? What are his or her habits? List the qualities of good writers.

_____

_____

_____

_____

_____

_____

_____

_____

_____

Now consider what it means to be a "good" reader—a reader who is independent, mature, and strong. What does a good adult reader do? What are his or her habits? List the qualities of good readers.

_____

_____

_____

_____

_____

_____

_____

_____

Take a look at your lists. They may include some of my ideas about good writers and readers.

Good writers:
* use writing as a tool for thinking.
* write often.
* have and use skills to craft and revise writing.
* observe the world closely.
* use writing for a variety of purposes.
* enjoy writing.
* have a sense of themselves as writers.
* take risks.
* read as writers.
* have an awareness of audience and different genres.

Good readers:
* read for meaning.
* integrate all three sources of information (meaning, semantics, and grapho-phonics).
* set goals for their reading in terms of length, variety, and time.
* read often and for a variety of purposes.
* use a full range of strategies to help them understand a text.
* are flexible in their use of strategies such as predicting and monitoring for meaning.
* use background experiences and prior knowledge to predict and confirm the text's meaning.
* evaluate what they've read.
* consider themselves readers.
* enjoy and appreciate reading.
* enjoy discussing and sharing reading experiences.

Becoming Readers and Writers

Irene Fountas and Gay Su Pinnell describe the goals for learning to read and write in their book, *Guiding Readers and Writers, Grades 3-6*. These goals are based on their understanding of what good, strong readers and writers do.

Learning to read in the fullest sense means developing decoding skills, but it also means much more. It means becoming readers who:

♦ read voluntarily and often.

♦ read a wide variety of materials.

♦ have confidence in themselves as readers.

♦ present themselves as readers to others.

♦ read to become informed on a wide range of topics.

♦ read to improve their lives.

♦ read to have satisfying and rewarding vicarious experiences.

♦ read to expand their world beyond the here and now.

♦ collect books and refer to favorites again and again.

♦ recommend books to others.

♦ talk with others about what they read.

♦ know authors and illustrators, genres, and styles.

♦ develop preferences and constantly expand them.

♦ reflect on their reading.

♦ make connections between and among the things they have read.

♦ think critically about what they read.

Learning to write in the fullest sense means more than developing composing and spelling skills. It means becoming writers who:

♦ write voluntarily and often.

♦ write in a wide variety of genres.

♦ have confidence in themselves as writers.

♦ present themselves as writers to others.

♦ use writing as a tool for thinking.

♦ write to communicate on personal and professional levels.

♦ write to share experiences or information with others.

♦ are sensitive to other writers, noticing techniques and styles.

♦ invite comments on, responses to, and critiques of their writing.

♦ draw on literary knowledge as a resource for their writing.

♦ use organized sets of information as a resource for their writing.

♦ explore favorite topics and genres.

As you consider your lists on page 12 and study the lists on pages 13 and 14, think about the implications for your classroom practice. If the ultimate goal is for our students to grow to be "good, mature" readers and writers, what needs to be happening in your classroom? What needs to be happening throughout the primary grades to create readers and writers who:

* believe they are capable of reading and writing?

* take risks and feel that they have a story to tell?

* realize that text carries meaning?

* want to read and write for authentic purposes?

* enjoy reading and writing?

If good, mature readers spend time reading, do we have enough time in our daily schedules for students to read? Are we giving them a chance through independent reading to try out the strategies we are teaching them? If we think good writers spend time revising their writing, are we giving our students enough time to write and revise, or are we doing all the revision for them? Do our students enjoy reading and writing even if they don't "know all of their letters and sounds" yet? Are they choosing their own topics for writing in order to feel invested in them? Do they feel like they are part of the "literacy club"? Are they being exposed to a variety of genres or are they simply filling in graphic organizers and writing to a pattern?

Matching Our Goals to Our Current Practices

Use this next exercise to help you think about how your current practices may or may not be fulfilling each attribute on your "good writers and good readers" lists. Write the good reader and writer attributes you listed earlier (and any you want to consider from the charts on pages 12 and 14) in the left column of the chart on page 17. Then take some time to think about examples from your current practice that support these attributes, and write them in the column on the right. Here is an example of how your chart for writing might look:

Good Writers	Examples from My Current Practice
Write often	My classroom environment promotes opportunities for kids to write for a variety of purposes, there are notepads and pencils in many areas.
Use writing for a variety of purposes	My second graders write fiction. They wrote a letter to the editor about fixing the bridge on Mill Road.
Take risks	Tim wrote a poem about his uncle dying and read it to the class. He wouldn't have done that earlier in the year. (The classroom environment and sense of community supports risk taking.)
Read as writers	I don't do enough with this concept. Next year, I'd like to use picture books more to model this good-reader habit. Perhaps an author study with a focus on craft?

Be tough on yourself as you reflect on your current practices. For example, if you find yourself jotting down "enjoy reading" under the left-hand column and "made Brown Bear, Brown Bear puppets" in the right-hand column, pause and reflect: *Did making the puppets truly help the students enjoy reading more? Did it advance any of the readerly goals I have for them?* There is nothing inherently wrong with making puppets. But if we ask children to make puppets during reading time, and then claim we don't have enough time to schedule independent reading and read aloud, then we're not being intentional in our teaching. Making puppets takes a lot of time.

By doing this brief exercise, you have tapped into the essence of effective planning—to continually articulate the outcomes you want for your students and put them "side by side" with your teaching practices to see if what you do in the classroom truly lives up to your goals. Now let's take a closer look at intentional teaching.

Does My Practice Measure Up?

Good Writers   **Examples From My Current Practice**

_____

_____

_____

_____

_____

_____

_____

_____

_____

_____

_____

_____

_____

Good Readers   **Examples From My Current Practice**

_____

_____

_____

_____

_____

_____

_____

_____

_____

_____

_____

_____

Intentional Teaching

> intend: The Latin verb *intendere* had a variety of metaphorical meanings, some of which have come through into English. Principal among them was "form a plan or purpose." —*Dictionary of Word Origins*

Teachers tell me all the time about new ideas they can't wait to try out. They love the ideas at first, but after a while, the appeal dies out. The teachers become bored and so do the students. There is no energy left. I believe this happens because, too often, we are not intentional when we choose to do something. We think we are when we study letter writing in February for Valentine's Day, or apples in the fall, or haiku poetry during a Japan unit, but that is theme teaching. I used plastic dinosaur-shaped counters during math when our theme of the month was dinosaurs. It was a cute idea, but it didn't help me meet my goal of teaching students more about dinosaurs. I am not implying that theme teaching is always unintentional. Of course, it can be rich and rigorous. But it is important to remember that *teaching* reading and writing is different than *using* reading and writing to learn content. We need to teach students to use writing and reading to learn content. And we need to be intentional in our planning of reading, writing, and content areas. We can ask students to write research projects during science, using the writing to help them learn the content, but we will also continue to focus on teaching the *writer* during writing workshop, where students choose their own topics.

Intention in Reading Workshop

It's important to think about what students need to learn from each unit in a reading and writing program. If they are learning how to "monitor for meaning" in reading, for example, I list my goals. Then I integrate the goals into my reading workshop. I model monitoring during read aloud. I look for evidence of monitoring while conferring during independent reading. My assessment method helps me to notice if students are monitoring for meaning. I incorporate monitoring strategies into homework and have students practice them in guided reading groups and shared reading sessions. This is very different from choosing a topic to cover or teaching a theme like "friendship" across the disciplines.

Intention in Writing Workshop

It's the same with writing workshop. We need to consider the components of our program (mini-lessons, independent writing time, materials, and share sessions) and then decide whether or not they support whatever we are studying. Teaching writing is not magical. It is not easy either. The hardest part is coming to feel that we know what we're doing. Some of us give students activities, topics to write about, or prompts to write from and call that writing workshop. Some of us teach students a "magic pattern" and call that writing instruction.

Other teachers have gotten the impression that workshop teaching is simply letting students write and write without worrying about spelling and grammar. They've seen "writing workshop" and don't want to try it because they don't think it provides enough instruction. However, if you are not intentionally teaching the writers during a writing workshop, those writers won't learn about spelling, grammar, or craft. One of the essential components of a writing workshop is "teaching." A gimmick or pattern may help us feel like we're doing *something* but I find that when students are taught a pattern, all the writing has the same inauthentic tone. Being intentional and planful gives us a true sense of confidence. When we feel in control and confident, we're more comfortable allowing for spontaneity and creativity, and our students learn to *really* write.

Planning for the Year Ahead

Being intentional in your teaching is a little like taking on a construction project. When my husband and I decided to put an addition on our house a while back, we started by having an architect create a plan. We spent lots of time discussing our needs and wishes before sketches were drawn. Even with the finished plans, as the builders began tearing down and reconstructing portions of our house, we requested changes. The original plans were added to and modified, almost daily. The builder joked that he was going to buy me a T-shirt that read "Might as well, while we're at it." Just like in teaching, having a plan helped us keep our eyes on our goals. But, there was always room for changes.

Katie Wood Ray refers to that as the "slightly out-of-hand feeling" in workshop teaching. And teachers generally don't like that feeling. We are taught that we must be "in control" at all times. (I remember that while student teaching, I was told that I should never smile for the first two weeks of school so that I would let the students know "who is in charge" of the class. Yikes! Can you imagine?) Being intentional helps us feel comfortable when things get slightly out of hand. We can follow the students' leads when we discover, for example, that they want to learn more about poetry or that they need more time on editing, because we have the big picture in mind and a monthly focus. We're able to allow for more individualized instruction within the context of the big picture because we've planned how to get to everything we must cover in the curriculum.

By spending some time planning the year, you will become organized. You'll feel in control and be spontaneous and creative along the way. Leave room for new discoveries, interests, and needs. You want to feel comfortable saying "might as well, while we're at it," knowing that you are only enhancing the original plan, not leaving something out. This is what we mean by the art of teaching. The students' interests and abilities, current events, and new learning from professional development will all influence your plans for the year. Keep this in mind while working to put it all together.

Intentional Planning

Planning curriculum based on our goals isn't only about the work we and our students are doing. We must consider all the components of an effective primary classroom:

* assessments
* materials
* room organization
* schedules
* flexible grouping of students

Assessing Students Intentionally

When I began teaching, I thought of assessment as something that came at the end of a unit, after I had covered a part of the curriculum. I tested the children to see if they "got it." But when my focus shifted from worrying about what I was going to cover to what I noticed the children doing in reading and writing, it became clear what I needed to teach. I didn't need to rely so heavily on the teacher's manuals.

Being a Learner of Teaching

In her book, *On Solid Ground: Strategies for Teaching Reading, K–3,* Sharon Taberski helps us think about being intentional when teaching reading strategies. Hers is yet another voice reminding us that we need to first be learners of teaching. She asks us to consider these questions:

- ◆ Are you using your time well?

- ◆ Have you established goals and created the supports that enable you to be successful?

- ◆ Are you making connections among all the things you do?

- ◆ Does your day make sense for you and your children?

Sharon has spent years learning to think of her teaching systematically—about how the components of the day, her goals for literacy teaching, and her role as teacher work together. She says that creating plans for a comprehensive, balanced literacy program—being intentional in our teaching—is about much more than just deciding *what* to teach. It's about naming our goals for students and making sure all the components of our program (reading and writing workshops, read aloud, independent reading, assessments, homework, small-group instruction, whole-group instruction, and individual instruction) support those goals. It's hard work. But the payoff is huge. Sharon says it best:

> *"Gone are the days when I leave my classroom exhausted and overwhelmed by countless and often contradictory demands. I'm no longer worn out from 'pushing and pulling' children through unconnected activities that others say are good for them. I know what I want to happen and I'm clear about my role in helping children. And I assess my teaching and children's learning continuously, so I can do more of what's working and less of what isn't."*

More recently, I joined the teachers at Roberts Avenue School in Danbury, Connecticut, to study assessment and to develop more meaningful ways of using it to drive instruction. In the process, we arrived at the following conclusions:

* We always begin with what the child knows.
* We value the process as much as the product.
* We encourage self-assessment.
* We believe assessment should be ongoing, objective, varied, open, honest, reflective, and integrated.

Assessment that is ongoing—before, during, and after a lesson—is extremely valuable when it comes to planning. As Richard Allington says, "When children write, you can see what they need to learn." And when we listen to children read and take careful notes on what they do, we see what they need to learn. Kenneth and Yetta Goodman call this "kid watching."

Dr. J. Richard Gentry, in his book *The Literacy Map*, reminds us of the importance of working quickly at the beginning of the school year to know all the students as individuals. He suggests we start by asking these questions about every student:

* Is the child reading independently?
* On what level is this child reading?
* What are his or her attitudes about books?
* How is this child coming along as a writer?
* What is he or she passionate about and how can I cultivate that passion in reading and writing?
* What words and patterns can this child spell?
* What important spelling work does this child need?

In the classrooms where I work, I encourage teachers to assess each student using questions like these during the first few weeks of school. I also urge them to administer a running record on each student to find out the strategies he or she is using. Writing workshop begins on the very first day (yes, even in kindergarten), which enables us to learn right away about each student and his or her views about writing. We also use a spelling assessment developed by J. Richard Gentry, which can be found in *The Literacy Map*, to get a baseline assessment of each student's understanding of conventional spelling patterns. The spelling test is administered three or four times during the school year and provides us with valuable information about each child, as well as ideas for group lessons.

Thoughts on Assessment

By carefully observing individual students in the course of ongoing classroom activities, we evaluate, reflect, and revise our instructional plans on the basis of what students do. We let students know when they are successful in a learning task, and provide the support they need to complete tasks they are yet unable to do on their own. Equally important, kid watching is a way for us to evaluate ourselves and our teaching.

—from Schulman and DaCruz, *Guided Reading: Making It Work* (Scholastic Professional Books, 2000)

Organizing Notes and Records

I spent many years in my own classroom developing and fine-tuning my assessment practices, using a wide variety of techniques and record-keeping tools including:

* anecdotal notes,
* running records,
* interviews, surveys, and inventories,
* concepts about print assessments,
* family interviews,
* observations during reading, spelling, writing, and speaking,
* conversations with children (conferences).

I used a three-ring binder for my long-term assessment records, with a tabbed section for each student. In it, I would store anecdotal notes, interview forms, spelling assessments, running-record forms, as well as math assessments and writing samples.

For daily assessment records, I kept a clipboard with a cover sheet that listed the entire class. After each student's name, I'd write the date when I held a conference with him or her. By glancing at the cover sheet, I could quickly see with whom I needed to meet on any given day. Under the cover sheet, I kept a form for each student. On the form, I listed anecdotal notes and quick running records taken during independent reading and writing. I could flip through the pages and get a sense of patterns of learning and needs in the class. For instance, if I flipped through the pages and noticed that eight or ten students needed work on punctuation or elaboration in writing, I knew what to focus on for the next mini-lesson in writing workshop.

About once a month or so, I placed the forms from the clipboard in the appropriate child's section in the assessment binder. I would then have everything together when it came time to write evaluations for conferences and report cards.

Many of the teachers with whom I now work use a similar assessment routine. Some of them use spiral-bound notebooks. Some use cards or sticky address labels on which they write notes and can place in a notebook later. I have never seen two teachers use exactly the same record-keeping method. There may have been similarities, but everyone modified routines to fit their own style and needs. The point is to have an assessment routine and a way to keep track of your assessments so that you can be intentional in using authentic assessment to drive instruction.

Are we pushing our kindergarten students?

Some kindergarten teachers with whom I've worked have associated authentic assessment in kindergarten with "a push toward more academics." Calling for authentic assessments in the primary grades is not about "pushing academics," though. It's about recognizing that children come to school with varying degrees of literacy knowledge. Some children come to school already reading. We need to find out what our youngest learners know right away so that we know what they need. Does it make sense for Michael to sit through a week of gluing M&Ms and marshmallows on an "M worksheet" (as I've seen in some kindergarten classes where they study a letter a week) if he already knows the letter M and its sound? Probably not. Authentic assessment in kindergarten is not about making sure all students are reading by the end of the year. It's about recognizing that some will be reading before the end of the year, and supporting all the learners in our rooms.

Determining Developmental Levels

Gay Su Pinnell and Irene Fountas offer two wonderful charts that outline the growth of readers and writers over time, from kindergarten to grade 6. (See pages 26 and 27.) They list developmental levels at the top of each column, characteristics of readers within each column, and approximate grade levels at the bottom of each column. As such, they encourage us to consider students first instead of grade level. I've included the charts for kindergarten to grade 6 because it's helpful to see where our primary students are headed. Also, in every primary class, there is always a wide range of reading and writing skills. It is not uncommon to find second grade students who are "self-extending writers or readers," which are described in the "Grades 3–4" column on the chart. You don't want to stop assessing a first grader just because he or she holds all of "first grade" characteristics.

Intentional assessment means finding out who our students are, regardless of their grade level. The teachers with whom I work have found charts like these helpful in figuring out where a particular student is and where he or she needs to go next. These charts are also helpful as starting points in matching students up with appropriately leveled texts.

When we think about assessment, then, we realize there is much more to it than what is mandated by the district two or three times a year for benchmarking purposes.

Using Materials Intentionally

If we want our students to consider themselves readers and writers, we must give them choices about the kinds of materials they use. For example, if we are teaching a poetry unit, it makes sense to offer different shapes and sizes of paper, particularly paper that is long and skinny. I have heard it said that "the material is the method." Choose wisely. If your goal is to create an environment where reading and writing

Supplies should be labeled, accessible, and centrally located.

Building an Effective Reading Process Over Time

Emergent Readers [Levels A–B]	Early Readers [Levels B–H]	Transitional Readers [Levels H–M]	Self-Extending Readers [Levels M–R]	Advanced Readers [Levels R–Y]
✳ Become aware of print. ✳ Read orally, matching word by word. ✳ Use meaning and language in simple texts. ✳ Hear sounds in words. ✳ Recognize name and some letters. ✳ Use information from pictures. ✳ Connect words with names. ✳ Notice and use spaces between words. ✳ Read orally. ✳ Match one spoken word to one printed word while reading 1 or 2 lines of text. ✳ Use spaces and some visual information to check on reading. ✳ Know the names of some alphabet letters. ✳ Know some letter-sound relationships. ✳ Read left to right. ✳ Recognize a few high frequency words.	✳ Know names of most alphabet letters and many letter-sound relationships. ✳ Use letter-sound information along with meaning and language to solve words. ✳ Read without pointing. ✳ Read orally and begin to read silently. ✳ Read fluently with phrasing on easy texts; use the punctuation. ✳ Recognize most easy high frequency words. ✳ Check to be sure reading makes sense, sounds right, looks right. ✳ Check one source of information against another to solve problems. ✳ Use information from pictures as added information while reading print.	✳ Read silently most of the time. ✳ Have a large core of known words that are recognized automatically. ✳ Use multiple sources of information while reading for meaning. ✳ Integrate sources of information such as letter-sound relationships, meaning, and language structure. ✳ Consistently check to be sure all sources of information fit. ✳ Do not rely on illustrations but notice them to gain additional meaning. ✳ Understand, interpret, and use illustrations in informational texts. ✳ Know how to read differently in some different genres. ✳ Have flexible ways of problem-solving words, including analysis of letter-sound relationships and visual patterns. ✳ Read with phrasing and fluency at appropriate levels.	✳ Read silently; read fluently when reading aloud. ✳ Use all sources of information flexibly in a smoothly orchestrated way. ✳ Sustain reading over texts with many pages, that require reading over several days or weeks. ✳ Enjoy illustrations and gain additional meaning from them as they interpret texts. ✳ Interpret and use information from a wide variety of visual aids in expository texts. ✳ Analyze words in flexible ways and make excellent attempts at new, multisyllable words. ✳ Have systems for learning more about the reading process as they read so that they build skills simply by encountering many different kinds of texts with a variety of new words. ✳ Are in a continuous process of building background knowledge and realize that they need to bring their knowledge to their reading. ✳ Become absorbed in books. ✳ Begin to identify with characters in books and see themselves in the events of the stories. ✳ Connect texts with previous texts read.	✳ Read silently; read fluently when reading aloud. ✳ Effectively use their understandings of how words work; employ a wide range of word-solving strategies, including analogy to known words, word roots, base words, and affixes. ✳ Acquire new vocabulary through reading. ✳ Use reading as a tool for learning in the content areas. ✳ Constantly develop new strategies and new knowledge of texts as they encounter greater variety. ✳ Develop favorite topics and authors that form the basis of lifelong reading preferences. ✳ Actively work to connect texts for greater understanding and finer interpretations of texts. ✳ Consistently go beyond the text read to form their own interpretations and apply understandings in other areas. ✳ Sustain interest and understanding over long texts and read over extended periods of time. ✳ Notice and comment on aspects of the writer's craft. ✳ Read to explore themselves as philosophical and social issues.
Texts: Simple stories with 1–2 lines.	*Texts:* Longer books with high frequency words and supportive illustrations.	*Texts:* Texts with many lines of print; books organized into short chapters; more difficult picture books; wider variety of genre.	*Texts:* Wide reading of a variety of long and short texts; variety of genre.	*Texts:* Wide reading of a variety of genre and for a range of purposes.
Approximate Grades: K–1	1–2	2–3	3–4	4–6

26

Building an Effective Writing Process Over Time

Emergent Writers	Early Writers	Transitional Writers	Self-Extending Writers	Advanced Writers
* Write name left to right.	* Write known words fluently.	* Spell many words conventionally and make near accurate attempts at many more.	* Spell most words quickly without conscious attention to the process.	* Understand the linguistic and social functions of conventional spelling and produce products that are carefully edited.
* Write alphabet letters with increasingly accurate letter formation.	* Write left to right across several lines.	* Work on writing over several days to produce longer, more complex texts.	* Proofread to locate their own errors, recognize accurate parts of words, and use references or apply principles to correct words.	* Write almost all words quickly and accurately, and fluently.
* Hear and represent some consonant sounds at the beginning and ends of words.	* Write 20 to 30 words correctly.	* Produce pieces of writing that have dialogue, beginnings, and endings.	* Have ways to expand their writing vocabularies.	* Use dictionary, thesaurus, computer spell check, and other text resources; understand organization plans for these resources.
* Use some letter names in the construction of words.	* Use letter-sound and visual information to spell words.	* Develop ideas to some degree.	* Understand ways to organize informational writing such as compare/contrast, description, temporal sequence, cause/effect.	* Control a large body of known words that constantly expands.
* Sometimes use spaces to separate words or attempted words.	* Approximate spelling of words, usually with consonant framework and easy-to-hear vowel sounds.	* Employ a flexible range of strategies to spell words.	* Develop a topic and extend a text over many pages.	* Demonstrate a large speaking and listening vocabulary as well as knowledge of vocabulary that is used often in written pieces.
* Label drawings.	* Form almost all letters accurately.	* Consciously work on their own spelling and writing skills.	* Develop pieces of writing that have "voice."	* Notice many aspects of the writer's craft in texts that they read and apply their knowledge to their own writing.
* Establish a relationship between print and pictures.	* Compose 2 or 3 sentences about a single idea.	* Write in a few different genres.	* Use what they know from reading texts to develop their writing.	* Critically analyze their own writing and that of others.
* Remember message represented with letters or words.	* Begin to notice the author's craft and use techniques in their own writing.	* Demonstrate ability to think about ideas while "encoding" written language.	* Recognize and use many aspects of the writer's craft to improve the quality of their writing.	* Write for a variety of functions— narrative, expressive, informative, and poetic.
* Write many words phonetically.	* Write about familiar topics and ideas.	* Use basic punctuation and capitalization skills.	* Write for many different purposes.	* Write in various persons and tenses.
* Write a few easy words accurately.	* Remember messages while spelling words.	* Continue to incorporate new understanding about how authors use language to communicate meaning.	* Show a growing sense of the audience for their writing.	* Write for different audiences, from known to unknown.
* Communicate meaning in drawing.	* Consistently use spacing.		* Critique own writing and offer suggestions to other writers.	* Write about a wide range of topics beyond the present time, known settings, and personal experiences.
	* Relate drawings and writing to create a meaningful text.			
	* Reread their writing.			
Text: Simple labels and sentences with approximated spelling.	*Texts:* One or more sentences around a single idea on a few pages; some conventionally spelled words.	*Texts:* Longer texts with several ideas; mostly conventional spelling and punctuation; simple sentence structure.	*Texts:* A variety of genres; conventional use of a spelling and punctuation; more complex sentence structure; development of ideas in fiction and nonfiction, use of a variety of ways to organize nonfiction.	*Texts:* A variety of long and short compositions; wide variety of purpose and genre; literary quality in fiction and poetry; variety of ways to organize informational text.
Approximate Grades: K-1	1–2	2–3	3–4	4–6

Materials for K-2 Reading and Writing Workshops

- an extensive classroom library with reading materials in a variety of genres and formats (such as poetry, nonfiction, lists, recipes, magazines, and songs) and on a variety of topics, displayed with covers facing out, inviting readers to enjoy them
- reading material that reflects your intended units of study
- leveled reading material and individual baskets or bags for independent reading:
  - easy-reading material
  - instructional materials that allow students to practice reading strategies
  - challenging material
- a place for young writers to keep their writing, such as a filing system for long-term work and folders or notebooks for short-term work
- individual spelling resource books and lots of reference charts around the room to promote independence
- writing supplies in a centrally located area or on each table for small groups to share

for authentic purposes will take place, students need access to real books and real writing tools, as well as real reasons to read and write.

The materials you use will change over time, as your intentions change. Be thoughtful. If you know, for example, that your plan for next month is to study nonfiction, you can pepper your library with nonfiction materials two weeks before you even introduce the term to your students. Students will discover the materials and, perhaps, notice things to bring to the discussion at the beginning of your study.

Children who come to school with a strong knowledge of letters and sounds, concepts about print, and reading strategies are fortunate. Many of them have had exposure to great stories and authentic reasons to read and write. They often have their own books at home and collections of pens and markers to write greeting cards and stories. But what about students who aren't so fortunate? Take a few minutes to list ways the materials in your classroom help you support literacy. Consider what you can do to make sure all children have access to and knowledge of how to use the materials in your room independently.

_____

_____

_____

_____

_____

_____

_____

_____

Magazines for Primary Libraries

American Girl *(www.americangirl.com/agmg/index.html)*

Boys' Life *(www.boyslife.org)*

Cricket *(www.cricketmag.com)*

Dig *(www.digonsite.com)*

Kids Discover *(www.kidsdiscover.com)*

Ladybug *(www.cricketmag.com)*

Muse *(www.musemag.com)*

Ranger Rick *(www.rangerick.com)*

Scholastic News *(www.scholasticnews.com)*

Spider *(www.cricketmag.com)*

Sports Illustrated for Kids *(www.sikids.com)*

Your Big Backyard *(www.nwf.org/yourbigbackyard)*

How to Get Them

◆ Request gift subscriptions from parents.

◆ If you and your colleagues subscribe to different magazines, share.

◆ Ask the librarian for back issues to add to your classroom library.

Materials Checklist

Ask yourself: Which materials do I have? How can I get the materials I need?

___ alphabet charts

___ alphabet rubber stamps

___ Big Books and sets of little books

___ Big Book stand

___ books, newspapers, and magazines that represent the range of readers in your class

___ books with tapes (Have parent volunteers tape stories at home.)

___ chalk and small chalkboards

___ charts and stories written during shared writing

___ class-made charts

___ clipboards

___ computer and printer with software for word processing

___ dictionaries

___ envelopes

___ flannel board

___ glue

___ individual book baskets (to hold books for independent reading)

___ labels for objects/artwork on display

___ magnetic letters

___ overhead transparencies

___ paint easel and supplies

___ paper in a variety of sizes, textures, and colors

___ pens, crayons, and pencils

___ pocket chart (for rereading, reconstructing, and innovating on texts)

___ poem, song, and nursery rhyme charts

___ postcards

___ pre-made books (Parents and volunteers love to do these, too.)

___ puppets

___ sand trays

___ science table

___ stamps to indicate "draft" papers and date

___ staplers

___ stickers

___ sticky notes

___ tape recorder and earphones

___ thesaurus

___ typewriter

___ washable markers and pens

___ word cards

—adapted from *Primary Purposes: Getting Started*, Fairfax County Schools, Fairfax, Virginia Department of Instructional Services

A large meeting area with easy access to reading materials, writing folders, and supplies.

Organizing Our Space Intentionally

In her book, *In the Company of Children*, Joanne Hindley quotes her friend and colleague Isabelle Beaton: "Geography is everything. I realized that I needed to figure out what I wanted to happen and how my classroom geography could support and enhance—or inhibit and deter—those goals. A country's geography predetermines a lot of what goes on in that country—for example, rivers and mountains form natural barriers and then people/society put up others: a railroad cut, a highway, a wall. But in my classroom I determine the geography. I can put up barriers to communication *or* I can set things up to encourage conversation. I can establish lonely islands of I's *or* I can form communities and provinces of we's. Everyone can have his or her own of each thing *or* groups can share. All the energy in my room can come from me *or* I can have constellations of energy. And the geography I put in place will do that for me."

Think carefully about how your room needs to look in order to allow comfortable space for whole-group, small-group, paired, and individual work. In the following sample floor plans, notice the:

 * large and small spaces for whole- and small-group work,

 * areas for group and individual work,

 * areas for quiet and noisy activities,

* adequate storage for group and individual items,
* clearly labeled work areas and materials,
* materials, organized for easy access,
* classroom library.

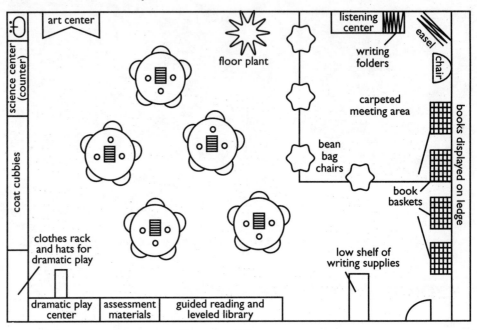

An ideal kindergarten classroom

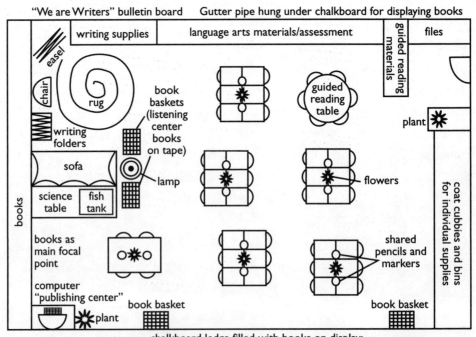

An ideal first- or second-grade classroom

The arrangement of the classroom can facilitate learning and promote literacy. For example, children write letters when there is stationery in the writing center. They expand their knowledge of science topics when there are appropriate books at the science table. They explore different genres when there is a range of books in the classroom library. We create this kind of environment by providing:

* areas that interest and challenge children, such as an interactive science table, a letter-writing table, a listening center, and a poetry center

* multiple locations for writing tools and reading materials

* books placed strategically to complement areas of study and to invite browsing

* displays that encourage talk, reading, and writing, such as interactive bulletin boards and pocket charts

* materials that make it easy to respond to literature, such as sticky notes, bookmarks, sign-up sheets for book talks, and a bulletin board for recommendations

* areas for quiet reading

* areas for group work

If you take a look inside some of the most progressive classrooms, you may notice that they look a little like a living room. If we think back to our beliefs about good readers and writers from earlier in this chapter, it's easy to see why. Where do we as good readers and writers spend time reading and writing? Most likely, we find a comfortable place to be at home—we don't necessarily go to a desk or office-like area. I love to visit classrooms that have artwork, lamps, a sofa, a carpet, and plants. These touches set a tone that respects the literacy learning taking place there. A classroom with them says, "You are welcome to feel comfortable while learning here."

When I asked first-grade teacher Kathy Hamilton to describe her "ideal room," she told about the bookshelves and comfortable seating areas and then, glancing around her current classroom, she admitted, "Everything you don't see here. I really need to think more about my classroom environment and the messages I am sending." She then proceeded to sketch a map of her classroom and the changes she planned on making. "Don't you think the library will look great here? It will be the first thing the kids see when they walk in the room.

Sketch Your Ideal Classroom

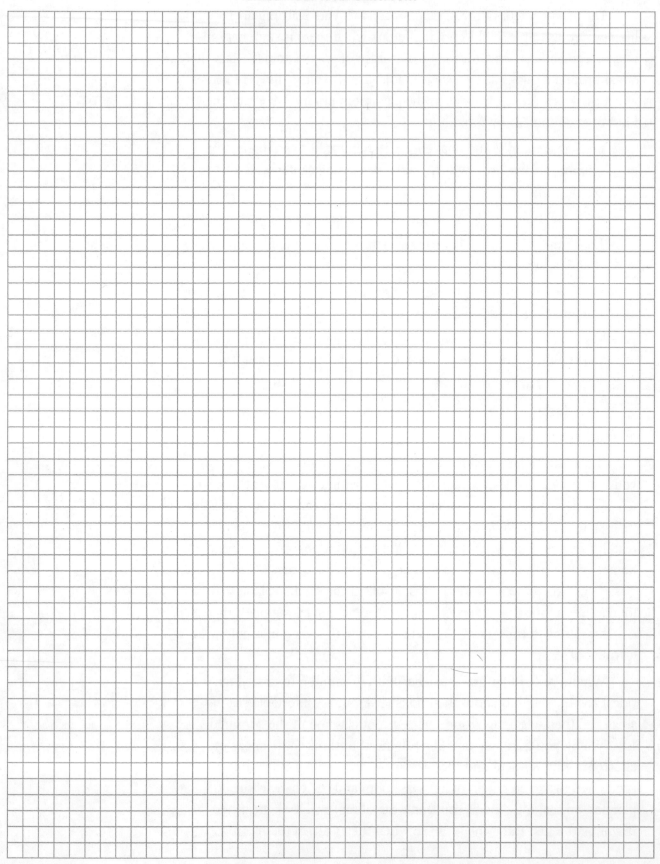

How about a sofa over here?" By considering the intentional use of her classroom space, Kathy saw her room from her students' point of view and created an environment that invited literacy learning in a "real-world" setting.

Take some time now to sketch out your ideal room, using the graph paper on the previous page. Include the following elements:

* whole group work space and a meeting area

* small group work space

* independent work space

* centrally located materials which support independence

* prominently displayed, easily accessible library

* learning centers such as writing, science, and math

Experiment with your room layout. Can you place the furniture so that it will help you meet your intentions for literacy development? If you don't have a room-size carpet, can you use carpet samples? (These can be obtained from any carpet store for a minimal fee, sometimes for free.) I find it helpful to sketch my ideal room layout before moving any furniture.

Creating Our Schedules Intentionally

Time. There is a finite amount of it in any school day, any school year. If our schedules match our goals, though, we make the best use of the limited amount of time we have. We give students the time they need to become involved with reading, writing, speaking, and listening.

The Daily Schedule

What does a daily schedule for workshop teaching look like? I offer the example on the next page from when I taught first grade. (For several other examples, read the professional books listed on pages 67 and 68.) You may feel you can't create a schedule like this one, given the large uninterrupted blocks of time for reading and writing. But think of it as the ideal to reach towards.

The first few minutes of the day set the tone for literacy learning. Instead of doing busywork, I moved among students while they were reading self-chosen material. I was able to touch base with students

TEACHER TIP

If you are working with a group of colleagues, visit each others' rooms to offer feedback and suggestions about room layout, aesthetics, and materials based on the criteria spelled out in this section.

First Grade / SCHEDULE FOR READING AND WRITING

8:50–9:05 **Independent Reading**
- The children arrive and take out their independent reading material. I confer with students and sometimes meet briefly with a small group.
- Trained parent volunteers read with students who don't have strong support at home.

9:05–9:20 **Read Aloud**
- I always try to start our day with a read aloud. Sometimes it is related to seasonal or current events, sometimes I reread an old favorite. Often it is linked to our inquiry studies in social studies or science.
- This time is also used for shared writing or shared reading, again usually tied into a content area.

9:20–10:30 **Reading Workshop**
5-10 minutes for whole-group focus lesson
45-50 minutes for independent reading and reading groups
10 minutes for share time
- I try to meet with two to three guided reading groups. The reading consultant in our building works in my classroom during part of this time. She often meets with an additional group.
- Students read independently and, eventually, in book discussion groups.
- Reading workshop ends with a share session focusing on process.

10:35–11:20 **Special**: Art, Music, Physical Education, or Media

11:30–12:30 **Lunch/Recess**

12:35–1:25 **Writing Workshop**
5-10 minutes for whole-group focus lesson
30 minutes for independent writing
10-15 minutes for share time
- I gather students at the carpet and lead into my writing lesson (which often includes a read aloud), and then send them off for independent writing time. I confer with individuals and small groups during this time.
- Writing workshop ends with a share session focusing on process.

1:30–3:00 **Math and Inquiry** (rotating monthly with science and social studies)

3:00–3:15 **Read Aloud**
- I try to end the day reading from a chapter book.

with whom I needed to meet every day for extra support. Parent volunteers came in during this time, too, to read with individual students. It was an especially powerful use of time for children who didn't get a chance to read at home the night before.

During the 9:20 to 10:30 block, I held reading conferences or guided reading groups. For guided reading, I usually grouped students by reading level, but not always. Sometimes it made sense to group them because they needed support with a particular strategy, regardless of their reading level. After all, students at any level can struggle with choosing "just right" books or using the pictures as clues.

I held share sessions at the end of both reading and writing workshop. I learned from Sharon Taberski to ask the children to focus on their reading and writing process, and on their use of strategies, rather than on the product (reading a piece aloud, for example). Our share sessions began, like Sharon's, with a simple question: "What have you learned about yourself as a reader/writer today?" or "What are your plans for your reading/writing?"

This schedule provided time for large-group, small-group, and individual instruction. It allowed numerous opportunities for reading to children, reading with children, and reading by children. The reading and writing workshop blocks provided ample time for students to write, read, confer, share, and listen.

The Weekly Schedule

I find it helpful also to think of scheduling in terms of a whole week. Diane Snowball, a well-known educator from New Zealand (the country with the highest literacy rate in the world) and author of several books including *Spelling K–8*, asks us to consider a week of literacy learning from a student's perspective, that contains:

* at least four hours of reading fiction and nonfiction texts,

* at least one hour of writing or reading poetry,

* at least four hours of writing, which includes personal narratives as well as content area writing,

* two or three 20- to 30-minute reading groups with teacher involvement,

* special instruction in physical education and the arts,

TEACHER TIP

These schedules assume a full school day. If your kindergarten is a half day, you will have to make appropriate modifications. It's important to give as much time as you can to literacy development and use the time you do have intentionally, making sure you are not wasting a moment.

* between five and six hours of content area study in math, science, and social studies,

* between two and three hours of language/word study.

Take some time now to revise your schedule, using the sheet on the next page. Is there a 90- to 180-minute block of time for literacy instruction every day which includes small-group, whole-class, and individual reading and writing instruction? How much time are the students actually spending engaged in real reading during the day? Are there opportunities for independent reading of self-selected materials, for a sustained period of time? (You might want to build up from 10 minutes to over 30 minutes a day.) How much time is there for writing for a variety of purposes and writing of various types?

Grouping Students Intentionally

In her book, *Great Grouping Strategies: Dozens of Ways to Flexibly Group Your Students for Maximum Learning Across the Curriculum*, Ronit Wrubel reminds us that our planning needs to "take into consideration how the children will perform their tasks, and with whom they'll be working." When we talk about groups in reading and writing workshops, we don't mean groups based on ability or reading level. Group children by what you notice about them as readers and writers, and how you can get closer to teaching them what they need. For example, you may have a group of students who need work on "chunking" words or using picture clues. Maybe you have a few students who need help adding details to their writing or choosing topics to write about. These groups should be flexible and change all the time. And they shouldn't be named, because labels imply that they are long-term and stagnant.

Ronit Wrubel goes on to describe and analyze the hierarchy of grouping options, beginning with whole-class work and ending with individual work. Consider these options while planning reading and writing workshops:

* Whole Class: meeting times, read alouds, focus lessons, shares

* Cooperative Learning Groups: literature groups, learning centers

* Small Task, Skill-Specific, or Study Groups: guided reading, word study, writing

* Informal, Lesson- or Project-Based Groups: reading, writing

Scheduling Sheet

List changes you plan to make after reflecting on intentional scheduling. Is there a balance of reading and writing experiences which include reading and writing to children, reading and writing with children and reading and writing by children? Use this space to work on your ideal schedule which reflects your intentions.

Time Block **Teaching Activity**

* Socialization and Friendships

* Partnerships: writing, editing, and revision; reading

* Individual Work

—adapted from *Great Grouping Strategies* by Ronit Wrubel
(Scholastic Professional Books, 2002)

We need to teach our students how to interact within all groups, regardless of their size. Time spent modeling, role playing, and discussing different ways to work together in groups will pay off. Your classroom will run more smoothly, allowing you the time and space to confer with small groups or individuals. And be sure to listen in on groups to hear what students are saying to each other. You will gain an understanding of what they know and whether or not your teaching is "sticking."

 Intentional Teaching Begins With Intentional Planning

By reflecting on what you're after when teaching reading and writing, you have taken the first steps to becoming intentional in your planning. By defining your goals for your students, you are better able to analyze your classroom practices, including your assessment, scheduling, and grouping practices; your use of materials; and your classroom organization. Next, we will consider planning the curriculum.

Creating Curriculum Binders

You will be creating yearly, monthly, and daily plans for your reading and/or writing workshops. These plans will grow directly from the work you've done in this chapter, which is your analysis of your current literacy practices. I will show you how to create year-long plans and then how to translate those plans into monthly and daily plans. In the end, you will create a document which will be organized and housed in a three-ring curriculum binder. (In fact, you may want to get a jump start on your binder by making photocopies of the schedules, floor plans, and material lists in this chapter, and of the planning forms throughout the book.)

But first, we turn to Chapter 2 and take a closer look at current suggestions for best practices in literacy teaching. As you read, consider your year-long goals for your students.

2

Comprehensive Literacy Teaching

Best Practices to Consider for K–2

> "Education doesn't boil down to one particular set of books, curriculum or materials. Rather it is a philosophy that guides the selection of books, curriculum and materials."
>
> —Charlotte Mason

*I*n Chapter 1, you outlined your beliefs about what students need to become good readers and writers. Now let's take a look at what is considered current best practice in literacy teaching—teaching that isn't about a particular program or set of textbooks. As professionals, we need to be able to analyze curriculum and materials, and use them in the best ways possible. You are probably familiar with and applying many of these practices. I begin by defining the difference between *teaching reading and writing* and *developing readers and writers*. After that, I examine effective ways to develop the readers and writers in our primary classes.

Teaching Reading and Writing vs. Developing Readers and Writers

The following chart from *Creating Support for Effective Literacy Education* by Constance Weaver, Lorraine Gillmeister-Krause, and Grace Vento-Zogby shows the differences between teaching reading and developing readers:

Teaching Reading

1. The teacher uses a graded program with an anthology, workbooks and worksheets, and skills tests.

2. The program determines what will be taught and when it will be taught.

3. Children are grouped according to general ability and often remain in those groups for prolonged periods of time.

4. Children's reading is assessed with tests that accompany the basal or anthology.

Developing Readers

1. The teacher uses trade books for whole-class instruction and charts that all can see. Children also read trade books independently.

2. The teacher determines what will be taught and when it will be taught, based on professional knowledge and observation of and interaction with children.

3. Children requiring help may be grouped for specific kinds of instruction, but these groups are not permanent. They are flexible.

4. Children's reading is assessed in multiple ways, with attention to strategies used.

Teaching Writing vs. Developing Writers

How do you think the chart on page 42 would look if you substituted writing for reading? Use that chart to help you fill in your thoughts about writing.

Teaching Writing	**Developing Writers**

1 _____   **1** _____

_____   _____

_____   _____

_____   _____

_____   _____

2 _____   **2** _____

_____   _____

_____   _____

_____   _____

_____   _____

3 _____   **3** _____

_____   _____

_____   _____

_____   _____

_____   _____

4 _____   **4** _____

_____   _____

_____   _____

_____   _____

_____   _____

Using the New Standards to Guide Our Plans

If you're looking for guidance in developing readers and writers, check out *Reading and Writing Grade by Grade: Primary Literacy Standards* (also know as the New Standards), which recommends best practices in literacy teaching for grades K-3. It does not recommend any one program. It is a consensus document that represents years of conversation and debate among the nation's leaders in literacy teaching. Many experts at all points on the philosophical spectrum (Calkins, Taberski, Pinnell, Adams, Pearson, Giacobbe, and others) worked on the document for over two years with the Learning Research and Development Center at the University of Pittsburgh and the National Center on Education and the Economy, with support from the U.S. Department of Education. The result is a comprehensive, yet usable resource on literacy teaching that can help us plan instruction.

I love the New Standards because it offers well-rounded, practical advice. Expectations are listed for each grade, K-3, and are organized into six strands, three for reading and three for writing:

* Print-Sound Code   * Habits and Processes

* Getting the Meaning   * Writing Purposes and Resulting Genres

* Reading Habits   * Language Use and Conventions

The first-grade strand for "Getting the Meaning," for example, says: By the end of the year, we expect first-grade students to:

* notice whether the words sound right, given their spelling;

* notice whether the words make sense in context;

* notice when sentences don't make sense;

* solve reading problems and self-correct, through strategies that include using syntax and word-meaning clues, comparing pronounced sounds to printed letters, gathering context clues from surrounding sentences or pictures, and deriving new words by analogy to known words and word parts; and

* check their solution to a difficult word against their knowledge of print-sound correspondences and the meaning of the text.

The New Standards also lists examples of the types of books students should be reading at each grade level. It offers suggestions

for leveled independent reading books for each grade. The authors also discuss expectations for writing at each grade level. In general, they expect children in the primary grades to read books at their independent level and to write every day.

When I use the New Standards in my work with teachers, we are comforted by the fact that it doesn't represent any one person's point of view. It allows us to concentrate on understanding what a range of experts agrees upon as best practices. What I like best about this document is that it doesn't sell one program, book, or approach. Rather, it presents the best thinking of our day. Ten years from now the experts may tell us that some ideas have changed. And I hope they do, because that will mean new research has been conducted, which will lead to even better practices. After all, that's what today's accepted beliefs are—improvements of old ideas.

Think of astronomy. Practitioners in that field now have the Hubble telescope, which has helped them gain new knowledge about our solar system and come up with new questions, for example, "Is Pluto really a planet?" In literacy, we have more modern ways of assessing children, such as running records and Joetta Beaver's Developmental Reading Assessment. We also have more questions, for example, "How do we use the information from the DRA to create curriculum?"

Assessments like these give us new ways of thinking about how children read and write. They enable us to analyze children's use of strategies, for example, and really teach. We classroom teachers are being let in on the "secrets" that reading teachers have known for years. But with this knowledge comes responsibility—sometimes we are being asked to play the role of reading teachers. Therefore, we need tools to help us do our job, to help us to be intentional. Thinking about the "big picture" and creating a plan help us to be intentional.

I use the New Standards in my work as a consultant all the time. To obtain a copy, contact:

National Center on Education and the Economy (NCEE)
PO Box 10391
Rochester, NY 14610
(888) 361-6233
www.ncee.org

What Really Matters in Literacy Teaching?

Richard Allington reminds us to think of the obvious. Your completed curriculum binder, which you will create later with the help of this book, will remind you to stay focused on these truths. Students need to:

* read and write often.

* have access to books they can read.

* read and write fluently.

* become thoughtful readers and writers.

Students Need to Read and Write Often

Children need to read and write often for real purposes. The more they read and write, the better they get. The better they get, the more they like it and the more they do. The more they do, the better they get, and so it goes.

Literacy expert Diane Snowball once shared the results of a study by Anderson, Wilson, and Fielding that correlated the amount of time students spent reading with their standardized test scores. The students who scored in the 90th percentile spent an average of an hour or more a day reading. Although the subjects were fifth graders, there are implications for primary students. These habits need to be nurtured at the earliest grades.

Reading Volume of Fifth Grade Students and Levels of Achievement

Achievement percentile	Minutes of reading per day	Words per year
90th	57.4	2,357,000
50th	12.9	610,000
10th	1.6	51,000

Advice from the New Standards:
Read, Read, and Read Still More

Reading habits are as important as reading skills. Beginning in kindergarten, students need to read often—independently and with assistance—from the fiction, nonfiction, poetry, and prose genres. In the standards, "often" is quantified in these terms:

Kindergarten: Read or reread—independently or with another student or adult—two to four familiar books each day. Listen to one or two books read aloud each day at school and at home.

First Grade: Read—independently or with assistance—four or more books each day. Hear two to four books or other texts read aloud every day.

Second Grade: Read one or two short books or long chapters every day. Listen to and discuss every day one text that is longer or more difficult than what can be read independently.

    As you create your plans, refer back to these bottom-line recommendations to make sure that you are being intentional as you plan your day.

Diane Snowball shared another study that showed that the amount of time a student reads in school directly correlates with the amount of time he or she reads at home. In other words, a student will most likely read at home for the same amount of time he or she is expected to read at school. So, if we want children to read for a minimum of 60 minutes a day, they need to be reading material on their independent level (with 90% accuracy) for at least 30 minutes each day in school. The same could be said for writing.

What do students need to do well as readers and writers, and, consequently, as standardized test takers? They need stamina. They need to be able to interact with text on standardized tests for at least 45 minutes to an hour in one sitting. They need to be able to produce a volume of written material. Stamina is built up over time. At the beginning of kindergarten, for example, writing workshop may contain only ten minutes of independent writing time. But gradually, you should increase the amount of time, to give students the practice they need to write for longer periods.

To do well on standardized tests, students also need to know how to plan their writing and reading. They need to write with fluency and elaboration. They need to monitor for meaning and understanding as they read. These skills are best taught in a workshop environment where students are given large blocks of time to interact with print for real purposes.

> **To Do:** Review your schedule and think about the amount of time students are engaged in real reading and writing experiences. Do you need to make changes? If you are working with a group of colleagues, this is a perfect "homework" project. You may want to work in pairs, analyzing each other's schedules and offering feedback.

Students Need to Have Access to Books They Can Read

In the classroom in which I work, we use assessments such as running records and the DRA to find out how well our students are reading. Then we make sure we have plenty of books in our classroom libraries for the range of readers. Barbara Peterson's research on text characteristics, and how they support the use of strategies by beginning readers, is the basis for the book-leveling guidelines discussed in Calkins' *The Art of Teaching Reading* and Fountas and Pinnell's *Guided Reading*. Publishers are producing books according to Reading Recovery and Guided Reading levels. Teachers are coming up with their own systems—for example, sticking colored dots on their books which represent different levels. It doesn't really matter if you use letters, numbers, or colors. The point is to know the characteristics of the text and how they support young readers.

Marie Clay's Reading Recovery program taught us to look at texts differently. The text characteristics to consider when matching our youngest students—those emergent readers—with books are:

* **Size and style of print.** Larger, simpler print supports beginning readers.

* **Spacing of text.** Beginning readers need clear spacing to indicate individual words.

* **Placement of text.** Consistent placement of text on each page supports beginning readers—in later levels text may appear on different parts of a page.

* **Level of picture support.** In order to encourage the use of all strategies, pictures should reflect meaning of text in lowest levels of books.

* **Language structure.** Texts that contain language that sounds most like spoken language support beginning readers. They can tell what to expect. More literary language begins to appear in later levels.

Characteristics to consider for more proficient readers include:

* whether the sentences end on a page or wrap to the next page

* complexity of plot

* use of humor

* whether each chapter stands alone or all the chapters are connected to form one big plot

* number of characters

* use of referenced or non-referenced dialogue

* subject matter

To Do: If you are working with colleagues, bring some children's books to your next meeting. Together, analyze the books in relation to the text characteristics listed here. Decide which would work best for your students and discuss why.

Ways to Give Students Access to Books

Read Aloud

The New Standards reminds us that hearing books read aloud is the way young children most often engage in reading. But as they begin to crack the print-sound code, they can also read independently or, for harder texts, with assistance.

But even when students begin to read independently, read aloud should still be an important part of the day. According to the New Standards, when students read leveled books that are within their range for accuracy and fluency, they use only a fraction of the words and ideas they know. But through assisted reading and read aloud, they are exposed to new vocabulary and concepts that serve as a springboard to the next levels of competence.

When I taught full-time, I always read aloud to my students at least two or three times a day. If I returned to the classroom tomorrow, I would make every effort to read even more. I'd do my best to get through at least one chapter book every two or three weeks. I'd read shorter chapter books that look and feel like the books many first graders aspire to read by the end of the year. I'd also read longer chapter books at higher levels to improve my students' attention span and vocabulary. I'd reread old favorites. I'd reread sections of powerful pieces that moved the class the first time I read them. I'd read articles from magazines and newspapers. I'd read aloud much more than I ever did before.

The teachers with whom I work today face more and more required curriculum each year. Yet, they manage to fit in lots of read-aloud time. They manage this largely by reading aloud in all areas of the curriculum. As a result, they're finding that not only are the students' literacy skills growing, but the content of the curriculum is staying with them because they are building schema through the reading material.

Tips for Adding More Read Aloud to Your Day

◆ Read aloud during the first and last ten minutes of the day.

◆ Read aloud 20 minutes or more from a chapter book during a time of your choice.

◆ Occasionally read aloud during a mini-lesson, at the start of writing or reading workshop.

◆ Read aloud during transition times—the 15 minutes between lunch and physical education, for example.

◆ Read aloud "old favorites" during snack time.

◆ Read aloud nonfiction for five to ten minutes before a science, social studies, health, or math lesson.

◆ Have volunteers, specialists, or paraprofessionals read aloud to individuals or small groups.

◆ Cut out the busy work. (One teacher I know found a wealth of whole-class read-aloud time by cutting back on elaborate bulletin board projects.)

Reading aloud can build background knowledge, vocabulary, attention span, sense of story, and a love of literacy. My five-year-old son recently saw a photograph of Queen Elizabeth I in a *Kids Discover* magazine. He proceeded to tell me all about how Queen Elizabeth had black teeth because, "You know, Mommy, they didn't have good dentists in Shakespeare's time, and she wouldn't let any mirrors be in her palace because she didn't want to see her ugly smile." I was surprised by just how much he knew. When I asked him where he learned the information, he told me that his dad had read him *Stage Fright on a Summer Night* from the Magic Tree House series the night before. In it, there's a reference to Queen Elizabeth and her black teeth. Reading aloud builds background knowledge.

We all know that the students who have been read to regularly at home come to school with a huge advantage. We need to extend that advantage to all of our students. Reading aloud from a variety of texts (picture books, chapter books, poetry, nonfiction, letters, and so forth) is one of the most important things we can do.

To Do: If you are not familiar with Jim Trelease's *The Read Aloud Handbook*, you don't know what you are missing! In this beloved, classic guide, Trelease

* explains how reading aloud awakens children's imaginations and improves their language skills.

* shows how to begin reading aloud and which books to choose.

* discusses the latest research on reading to infants and using chapter books with preschoolers.

* suggests ways to create reader-friendly home, classroom, and library environments.

* gives tips on luring children away from the television.

* shows how to integrate silent reading with read aloud sessions.

* includes a treasury of more than 1,500 children's books that are great for reading aloud—from picture books to novels.

Look for this book in the library or bookstore and share it with your colleagues. Continue to add to your list of read alouds.

A Short List of Favorite Read Aloud Chapter Books for Primary Grades

As primary teachers, most of us have knowledge of and access to picture books. But what about chapter books? In the primary classrooms where I work, the teachers are often surprised and pleased when I introduce them. Most of the books in the following list are a part of a series. Often, I'll read aloud the first book in a series and tell the students that if they like it, they can find others from the series in the library or bookstore.

Marcel Ayme	*The Wonderful Farm*
L. Frank Baum	The Wizard of Oz series
Walter R. Brooks	Freddy the Pig series
Ann Cameron	*The Stories Julian Tells, Stories Huey Tells*
Eleanor Estes	The Moffats series
Janet Taylor Lisle	*The Lost Flower Children, Afternoon of the Elves, Gold Dust Letters*
Maud Hart Lovelace	Besty-Tacy series
Lensey Namioka	*Yang the Youngest and His Terrible Ear*
Edith Nesbit	*Five Children and It (and others)*
Mary Pope Osborne	Magic Tree House series
various authors	In Their Own Words series

Use the remaining blank lines to add some of your favorite read alouds.

_____

_____

_____

_____

_____

_____

_____

_____

_____

_____

If you're in a study group, share your list with the members of your group. You may want to bring examples of favorite read alouds to each meeting and begin with a short "book talk" where you introduce the book and why you think it makes a great read aloud.

Build a Classroom Library

Getting books into classroom libraries is a priority in the schools where I work. Teachers bring in books from home and scour tag sales, church sales, and library book sales. Parents donate books and give them as gifts. PTAs organize book swaps and fund-raisers to build classroom libraries. Administrators write grants to build classroom libraries. One teacher I know asks parents to "bid" on class-made books and uses the auction money to buy trade books. Publishers' book clubs, such as Scholastic's, are a wonderful way to build a library. Those bonus points can go a long way.

A classroom library organized by author and genre, with book covers facing out.

> ### *Five Ways to Get Books*
>
> **1.** Use book clubs and bonus points.
>
> **2.** Work with parents to hold benefit bake sales and auctions.
>
> **3.** Encourage books as gifts.
>
> **4.** Ask a local business to "adopt" the school.
>
> **5.** Research other possible sources of book funding, including local and federal governments, charitable organizations, service clubs, parent-teacher organizations, large companies, foundations, and individuals.

Your classroom library should contain fiction and nonfiction books to use in writer's workshop (i.e., "touchstone texts" that you refer to time and time again during the year), books that support independent reading, books for guided and shared reading, and books in a variety of genres. In addition to books, don't forget magazines.

Do you plan to level any of the books for your library? If so, perhaps with colleagues, decide on a leveling system, such as the one described in Irene Fountas and Gay Su Pinnell's *Guided Reading: Good First Teaching for All Children*. Only about a third of your existing library needs to be leveled to support independent and guided reading. However, it makes sense to level any new books that you acquire, even if they may not be housed in your library's independent or guided reading sections, to get a sense of how you might use them.

As you consider your library as a whole, sort the books into categories that support your goals and your students' needs and interests:

* books that expand children's literary experiences and introduce them to new genres and styles

* books that support research and inquiry

* leveled books that support children's reading development (The books you use for guided reading shouldn't go in the general class library. The books you use in shared reading will probably end up there, though, perhaps in a bin marked "Old Favorites.")

* books that are useful for reference, for learning content, or for browsing for general interest

* books for children to choose for independent reading

Our classrooms should be overflowing with books and material that students can and want to read. Keep a wish list. Do you need more poetry books for a writing genre study? Or could you use more "Level J" books for independent reading? If you have a list ready, when you are given some money (and told you must spend it by three o'clock that afternoon!) you can be intentional about what you purchase.

Create a Shared-Book Room

Many schools are creating shared-book rooms where teachers can sign out sets of books to augment their classroom libraries. Leveled books are purchased in sets of six or more and stored by level (based on Reading Recovery or Guided Reading levels) in a centrally located place in the school. These books are used in guided reading groups or with individual students. Leveled books that support content-area themes are also housed in a shared book room. Often, there are collections for use in writing workshop—books for a poetry genre study, for example, or books that have characters who write. Use caution, though, when

A well-organized, centrally located shared-book room.

creating a shared-book room; make sure funding and books aren't being drained away from classroom libraries.

Sharing books this way makes sense, since our goal is to get as many books into the classrooms as we can. Teachers can rotate books in their classroom libraries by sharing their collections with colleagues. It also makes sense when we consider the range of reading abilities among primary students. Books that are appropriate for some students at, say, the beginning of first grade, may also be appropriate for other students at the end of kindergarten. Gone are the days when each grade had "sacred" books that were only allowed to be taught in that grade. If we are focusing on teaching the reader, we shouldn't ask her to read a particular book in second grade if it is below her independent reading level. In other words, if she is ready to read *Ramona Quimby* in first grade, she shouldn't be reading it again for instructional purposes in later grades, because it will no longer be at her instructional level. She'll be ready for different material.

The biggest complaint I hear from literacy specialists about shared book rooms is that the books don't always "fly off the shelves." That's usually because teachers don't have the time to learn what's there. Keeping lists of what is available in the room will help to make teachers aware of what's available to them, and help them get into the habit of checking out books. Also, take note of the books that aren't being borrowed from the shared-book room—and ask yourself why. Was it leveled incorrectly? Leveling books is not an exact science. Some books just don't work for guided reading because the students don't have the necessary background knowledge or because the text does not adequately support the reader for another reason. If the book is not helpful in guided reading, it may make sense to take it out of the shared-book room and put it into a classroom library.

To Do: Take a tour of your classroom library. Are there books for all the types of readers in your room, or are there gaps? If you are working with a study group, tour each others' libraries. If your school has a shared-book room, make the effort to find out what is there.

Students Need to Read and Write Fluently

Marie Clay advises giving students "massive opportunities to interact with text at their level." We know that when students read word by word and struggle with phrasing, their comprehension suffers. Too much of their cognitive effort is deployed at the word and sentence level, and little remains for getting at the ideas, emotions, and images in the text. The key to fluency (and, therefore, comprehension) is matching students with books at their level, based on assessments such as the DRA.

Fluency in writing is equally important. The child who is overly concerned with perfect spelling will remain "stuck" trying to write a word rather than getting a whole idea down. Over time, with good daily habits and direct instruction in writing beginning in kindergarten, students can learn to write fluently. Fluency also comes with practice. Giving students lots of time to practice each day gives them a feeling of control over their reading and writing and increases their fluency. The key is to know where they are as readers and writers and to match them up with appropriate materials.

As you map out your year, consider when you'll administer different assessments for reading and writing fluency. Some assessments should be given at the beginning of the year and then repeated at different intervals, such as the DRA, running records, transitional spelling assessments, Concepts About Print, the Primary Language Record, and reviews of the students' writing portfolios. Most districts have mandates regarding assessment, but they don't always measure our vision of good literacy learning. We need to make sure that our assessments are giving us the best information possible in order to inform our instruction. Think "intentional."

Students Need to Become Thoughtful Readers and Writers

Reading and writing aren't just about figuring out those little black marks on the page. They are interactive processes involving decoding and encoding words, *and* constructing meaning.

We want students to become active, strategic readers as well as proficient decoders. We need to make sure our students understand what it means to be critical readers. In their book *Mosaic of Thought*, Ellin Keene and Susan Zimmermann say they "want children to develop the habits of mind of avid readers, to succeed in comprehending ever more challenging texts, and to use a wide variety of problem-solving strategies to remedy comprehension problems independently." They go on to describe the "proficient reader research" which confirms what you may have observed in yourself and in your students, namely that thoughtful, active, proficient readers are metacognitive: they think about their thinking during reading.

When we teach reading and writing, we can model our own

thinking and invite our students to make and share their own connections and thought processes. Kathy Hamilton, first-grade teacher at Roberts Avenue school, once shared these thoughts with me about modeling writing:

> I always thought I had to show them a perfect piece, so I spent so much time creating a "script" to share during the actual focus lesson time. I was afraid to model in front of the kids. What if I made a mistake? I'd have it all scripted. Then one day, I just wasn't prepared. I had to wing it! I created a piece of writing right in front of them, thinking out loud all the while. I made a few mistakes (not on purpose!) and the kids helped me come up with some words and phrases to use. It turns out, I modeled having the confidence to make a mistake . . . . Writing in my room changed after that day. Kids are less likely to worry about spelling and saying just the right thing, they just wing it. They know that writers sometimes make mistakes and it's okay to go back later and fix it up. They are much more likely to take risks now that I model risk-taking and thinking out loud. I think they have a clearer sense of what they are supposed to be doing during writing time.

Do you model your thought process during writing? How about during read aloud? Think about how you can use your shared writing and reading times to model active, strategic literacy.

Cambourne's Conditions for Learning

Teaching reading and writing should not be difficult. Most children seem to read in spite of what we, the adults in their lives, do to them. Frank Smith says that "learning is what people do best. If the conditions are right, learning comes easily." The difficult part of teaching reading and writing is sorting out what we really mean by "teaching reading and writing." What is our ultimate goal? How can we set up the right conditions so that learning comes easily?

The following chart helps us answer those questions. It comes from *Guided Reading: Making It Work* by Mary Browning Schulman and Carleen DaCruz Payne. They describe Brian Cambourne's conditions for learning and how they support components of a comprehensive literacy program. In the section following the chart, I'll explore those components more deeply.

Brian Cambourne, an Australian researcher, has studied and identified conditions for how young children learn to talk. Although children receive no formal lessons in talking, they have multiple opportunities every day to use and develop their language skills. They learn to speak in a very supportive and encouraging environment with many experienced and proficient language users. Cambourne believes these conditions are transferable to literacy instruction in the classroom (Cambourne, 1988).

Our own experience has demonstrated that Cambourne's conditions for learning apply to the acquisition of reading and writing skills. A language arts program that includes reading and writing *to*, *with*, and *by* children provides a rich environment for literacy growth. The following chart summarizes Cambourne's conditions for learning and shows how they may occur in a balanced literacy program.

Cambourne's Conditions for Learning	*How They May Appear in a Balanced Literacy Program*
Immersion	
Students are immersed in multiple opportunities to read and write that are purposeful and authentic throughout the day and across the curriculum areas.	A print-rich environment which includes read alouds of literature, some related to the content areas, and writing opportunities based on them, expand the possibilities for immersion. Learning centers provide a variety of purposeful and authentic literacy activities.
Demonstration	
Students have many demonstrations by teachers of the behaviors and strategies to use while reading and writing.	Shared reading, read alouds, shared writing, and guided reading allow for plenty of teacher modeling of reading and writing strategies.
Engagement	
Learners, at every level of proficiency, are active participants and are engaged in literacy activities.	Shared reading, shared writing, and guided and extension activities foster active participation of students at all levels.

Expectation

Teachers create a supportive classroom atmosphere that helps all students believe that they will learn to read and write.

Shared reading, shared writing, guided reading, and independent reading and writing times provide ways for children to be supported in their belief that they are readers and writers.

Responsibility

Students are given opportunities to make choices and are responsible for their learning through meaningful demonstrations and teacher support.

Literacy centers and independent work time allow students to choose their activities and be responsible for their performance and behavior. Individual reading and writing conferences help students evaluate their own learning and set goals.

Approximation

Students' best efforts with print in both reading and writing are encouraged and valued.

All teaching begins by acknowledging what students can do. Teachers accept students' levels and focus on developing strategies and skills one step at a time during shared reading, guided reading, shared writing, guided writing, and individual reading and writing conferences.

Employment

Students are given time, sometimes independently of the teacher, to use the reading and writing strategies they are learning.

Students practice their reading and writing strategies independently at literacy centers, during independent reading and writing times, and in guided reading groups.

Response

Teachers provide specific feedback or response while students are engaged in literacy activities, encouraging their continued success.

Prompts during guided reading, teaching points made after taking running records, and reading and writing conferences acknowledge what students do or need to do.

Although we have explained these conditions as separate items, they all work together and are interwoven daily into literacy learning in classrooms.

—from Schulman and DaCruz, *Guided Reading: Making It Work* (Scholastic Professional Books)

Components of a Comprehensive Literacy Program

> "Teaching is about loving questions and moving kids to search for answers. A great teacher gets excited about these unanswered questions and becomes an example of quest and curiosity. I admire teachers, but if they act like clerks, the kids won't get anywhere."
>
> —*Maxine Greene*

How can we make sure our students are reading and writing often, have access to books they can read, are gaining practice in reading and writing fluently, and are becoming thoughtful readers and writers? Through a comprehensive literacy program that is made up of these components:

Read Aloud	Word Work
Shared Reading	Writing Workshop
Independent Reading	Independent Writing
Guided Reading	Shared Writing/Interactive Writing

Read Aloud

Reading aloud to children is particularly valuable for those who are learning English as their second language or who have had limited experiences with print. Instructional assistants, parent volunteers, and older students can also read aloud to small groups or individuals in the classroom. For more on read aloud, see page 49.

Shared Reading

I love to observe Michele Masi teach during a shared reading session. She has such a gentle way with her students, but she also has high expectations. Michele often wisely chooses an "old favorite" for shared reading. "The bear went over the m . . ." she'll read while running a pointer under the words of the Big Book on the easel in front of the children gathered on the carpeted meeting area. As Michele's voice trails off, her first graders' voices get stronger and stronger. Even the most reluctant readers feel supported and encouraged enough to actively participate in this short, ten-minute shared reading experience.

Independent Reading

When I was first teaching, I had USSR time daily (Uninterrupted Sustained Silent Reading). My colleagues across the hall had DEAR time (Drop Everything and Read). Regardless of the name, these times were usually held during that extra fifteen minutes between gym and lunch. Or, children could read independently once they finished their "work" (worksheets or art project in response to a group story). I wasted a lot of time. In *The Art of Teaching Reading*, Lucy Calkins asks us to make independent reading central to our reading program.

When students are reading independently, we can catch a glimpse of what they are doing in their reading lives. We can explore whether what we are teaching during guided reading or shared reading is sticking. Independent reading gives students a chance to show us what they know. Find out what they know and use that to help them get to what they need to know next. Focus on the positives. During independent reading time, children are reading on their own or with partners from a wide range of material. Some reading is from a special collection at their reading level.

When I began moving among the children during independent reading to listen to them read and talk about their reading, I got a clearer picture of what I needed to teach. I was able to focus on their book choices. I noticed which strategies a child was using or not using. New ideas for focus lessons stemmed from their independent reading time.

According to *Primary Purposes*, a document published by educators in Fairfax County, Virginia, we support independent reading by:

- creating an attractive, inviting classroom library containing a range of reading materials,
- offering familiar or easy-to-read books as a reading option,
- providing adequate time to read,
- establishing clear expectations and guidelines for behavior,
- modeling independent reading behavior,
- introducing new books to the students through book talks,
- conferring with students about their independent reading.

Guided Reading

Kathy Hamilton meets with guided reading groups while her other students are reading independently. It is amazing to see how long those young children can stay focused during independent reading so that she can meet with groups. This doesn't happen by accident. Kathy spends a lot of time assessing her students using running records to match students up with texts for both guided reading and independent reading.

Kathy's guided reading groups are flexible. She changes configurations often, usually weekly. At the end of each week, she uses her assessment notes (such as running records and anecdotal records) to plan the next groups. She may group students with an eye toward teaching them a particular strategy, such as reading through the whole word to the ending or skipping an unknown word and reading beyond it to look for clues. The students may all be at different levels, working in different books.

Like many teachers, Kathy tries to work with two or three groups of three to six children a day. Usually, she gets independent reading started and then moves around the room among the students to make sure everyone is on task. Then, she gathers her first group. She positions groups so that she can keep an eye on the entire classroom while conducting guided reading.

Unlike in shared reading, Kathy does not read the text to the students first. Instead, she introduces the story, providing students with enough information to read the whole text independently, supporting them as they go and making teaching points during and after the reading. Multiple copies of the same book or story are often used. Guided reading gives students the opportunity to apply reading strategies to solve problems on unfamiliar texts.

Word Work

The teachers I work with spend 10 to 15 minutes a day focusing on particular vocabulary, spelling, and grammar issues. Issues are based on the needs of the class as determined in one-on-one conferences, in group work, and by reading the children's work. I used to use the time between recess and specials for word work. Of course, word work does not have to be isolated that way. By weaving it through the entire comprehensive literacy program, we give ourselves opportunities to help children notice and use letters and words. That knowledge is nurtured through the use of alphabet centers and word walls. There should always be some focus on vocabulary, spelling, and grammar during writing workshop, interactive writing, shared writing, and guided reading lessons. This work may include noticing and charting different patterns or sound-symbol connections (-*ing* words or *sh* words, for example). A good rule of thumb is to focus on helping children use what they know about words to read new words.

Writing Workshop

In writing workshop, students engage in writing a variety of texts on topics of their choice, with the teacher guiding the process by modeling, providing focus lessons, conferring, and giving them opportunities to share. Teachers encourage students to write in different genres and to improve the quality of their writing through revision and editing.

Independent Writing

Students write on their own, independent of the teacher, often in notebooks, on self-selected topics. Providing plenty of opportunities for children to write independently gives them the chance to use writing for different purposes across the curriculum.

Shared Writing or Interactive Writing

During whole-group interactive writing, the teacher "shares the pen" with the students, and elicits responses from them to create a text together. There are many ways to weave shared writing into our day. For example, many teachers don't write the morning message by themselves anymore, but with students as an interactive writing activity. Shared writing, like shared reading, gives students a chance to interact with print while being supported in an authentic way. Plus, we can steer the work so that it reinforces what's going on in another area of study, such as word work and writing workshop.

What Are the Implications for Classroom Practice?

The staff developers at Teachers College Reading and Writing Project, under the guidance of Lucy Calkins, developed some bottom-line expectations for good literacy instruction:

Writing Workshop: Bottom-Line Expectations

- Writing workshop happens *at least* four times a week in every classroom.

- Writing workshop lasts from 45 minutes to an hour and includes a focus lesson, workshop time, and sharing.

- Students write whole texts that carry their own thinking.

- There is a place to accumulate each child's writing (folders in grades K–2, notebooks in grades 2–5).

- Students' writing and books are visible, honored, and accessible around the room/school.

- Teachers read aloud every day from a variety of genres, also talking about each author.

- Teachers offer strategies for initiating and improving writing, noting what they see in students based on their growing knowledge (from rereading notes, articles, and professional development).

- Publication/celebrations are scheduled *at least* six to nine times a year and the dates are announced early in the year to administrators and parents.

Reading Workshop: Bottom-Line Expectations

◆ Each child reads books they can read with 90 percent accuracy for *at least* 30 minutes five times a week in school.

◆ There are at least 125 books in each classroom that the teacher thinks students can and will want to read. [I'd recommend even more . . . hundreds more.]

◆ About one third of the books in the classroom libraries are leveled.

◆ Teachers use running records plus observations and interviews to match students with books and to develop instructional plans and goals.

◆ Teachers help students choose books they can read with accuracy, fluency, and comprehension and help students sustain their reading.

◆ Children bring books they are working on between home and school.

◆ Phonics is used along with meaning when students encounter difficulty. (Additionally, 15 minutes a day are spent teaching chunks, word parts, alternate ways to spell a sound, and so forth.)

In this chapter, I asked you to consider the big picture. What is it we are really after when we are teaching children to read and write? In the next chapters, we will consider how we translate that big picture into a plan for the year.

To Do: Evaluate yourself in terms of comprehensive literacy teaching. Look again at the bottom-line practices listed on pages 65 and 66. How does your program measure up? What are your big questions about teaching reading and writing? Discuss them with colleagues. Read professional material to find answers to some of those questions. Study yourself as a reader and writer with an eye toward how you can use the information to teach your students.

Recommended Professional Reading List

What Really Matters for Struggling Readers: Designing Research-Based Programs by Richard Allington (Longman)

How's It Going?: A Practical Guide to Conferring with Student Writers by Carl Anderson (Heinemann)

A Fresh Approach to Teaching Punctuation: Helping Young Writers Use Conventions with Precision and Purpose by Janet Angelillo (Scholastic)

And With a Light Touch: Learning About Reading, Writing, and Teaching with First Graders, Second Edition, by Carol Avery (Heinemann)

The Art of Teaching Reading by Lucy McCormick Calkins (Longman)

The Art of Teaching Writing by Lucy McCormick Calkins (Heinemann)

The Early Detection of Reading *Difficulties* by Marie Clay (Heinemann)

An Observation Survey of Early Literacy Achievement by Marie Clay (Heinemann)

35 Rubrics & Checklists to Assess Reading and Writing by Adele Fiderer (Scholastic)

Thinking and Learning Together: Curriculum and Community in a Primary Classroom by Bobbi Fisher (Heinemann)

How Writers Work: Finding the Package That Works for You by Ralph Fletcher (Avon)

Live Writing: Breathing Life Into Your Words by Ralph Fletcher (HarperCollins)

Poetry Matters: Writing a Poem From the Inside Out by Ralph Fletcher (HarperCollins)

What a Writer Needs by Ralph Fletcher (Heinemann)

A Writer's Notebook: Unlocking the Writer Within You by Ralph Fletcher (Avon)

Craft Lessons: Teaching Writing K–8 by Ralph Fletcher and JoAnn Portalupi (Stenhouse)

Writing Workshop: The Essential Guide by Ralph Fletcher and JoAnn Portalupi (Heinemann)

Guided Reading: Good First Teaching for All Children by Irene C. Fountas and Gay Su Pinnell (Heinemann)

A Note Slipped Under the Door: Teaching from Poems We Love by Nick Flynn and Shirley McPhillips (Stenhouse)

The Literacy Map: Guiding Children to Where They Need to Be K–3 by J. Richard Gentry (Mondo Publishing)

Writing: Teachers and Children at Work by Donald H. Graves (Heinemann)

A Fresh Look at Writing by Donald H. Graves (Heinemann)

Strategies That Work: Teaching Comprehension to Enhance Understanding by Stephanie Harvey and Anne Goudvis (Stenhouse)

(continued)

For the Good of the Earth and Sun: Teaching Poetry by Georgia Heard (Heinemann)

Awakening the Heart: Exploring Poetry in Elementary and Middle School by Georgia Heard (Heinemann)

In the Company of Children by Joanne Hindley (Stenhouse)

Mosaic of Thought: Teaching Comprehension in a Reader's Workshop by Ellin Oliver Keene and Susan Zimmerman (Heinemann)

Spelling in Use by Lester Laminack and Katie Wood (National Council of Teachers of English)

After the End: Teaching and Learning Creative Revision by Barry Lane (Heinemann)

Dancing with the Pen by the Ministry of Education, Wellington, New Zealand (Richard C. Owen, U.S. Distributor)

Read to Write by Donald Murray (Harcourt Brace)

Write to Learn by Donald Murray (Harcourt Brace)

Nonfiction Craft Lessons: Teaching Information Writing K–8 by Joann Portalupi and Ralph Fletcher (Stenhouse)

What You Know by Heart: How to Create Curriculum for Your Writing Workshop by Katie Wood Ray (Heinemann)

Wondrous Words: Writers and Writing in the Elementary Classroom by Katie Wood Ray (National Council of Teachers of English)

The Writing Workshop: Working Through the Hard Parts (And They're All Hard Parts) by Katie Wood Ray with Lester Laminack (National Council of Teachers of English)

Your Classroom Library: New Ways to Give It More Teaching Power by Ray Reutzel and Parker Fawson (Scholastic)

Kids' Poems: Teaching Students to Love Writing Poetry, K–4, by Regie Routman (Scholastic)

Teaching Young Writers: Strategies That Work by Lola M. Schaefer (Scholastic)

Taking Running Records by Mary Shea (Scholastic)

Creating Classrooms for Authors and Inquirers, Second Edition, by Kathy G. Short and Jerome C. Harste with Carolyn Burke (Heinemann)

Joining the Literacy Club: Further Essays into Education by Frank Smith (Heinemann)

Spelling K–8: Planning and Teaching by Diane Snowball and Faye Bolton (Stenhouse)

Reading Process and Practice: From Socio-Psycholinguistics to Whole Language, Second Edition, by Constance Weaver (Heinemann)

Joyful Ways to Teach Young Children to Write Poetry by Jodi Weisbart (Scholastic)

You Kan Red This!: Spelling and Punctuation for Whole Language Classrooms, K–6, by Sandra Wilde (Heinemann)

3

Beginning Your Curriculum Binders

Using Units of Study to Plan Your Reading and Writing Workshops

"A place
for everything,
and everything
in it's place."
—unknown

T he process of putting together curriculum binders based on units of study (periods of focus on a particular genre or strategy) has been extremely rewarding for the many teachers with whom I've worked. Reading specialists, staff developers, and administrators also find value in working on a project like this. Once they've completed the process, they have two comprehensive curriculum documents, one for reading and one for writing, based on current best practices and the needs of their students.

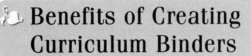 Benefits of Creating Curriculum Binders

Curriculum binders enable you to:

* integrate the required curriculum with current best practices.

* see clearly where you have been and where you are going next in your workshops.

* feel in control of your teaching while letting the students be central to the process.

* integrate new learning from professional reading, and staff development workshops into your plans, in an intentional manner.

* use your instructional time more intentionally, which will allow more time for independent reading and read aloud.

* transport materials easily for off-site planning sessions.

* share your organized plans easily with others.

* see the big picture and focus on your needs for materials, books, and professional development.

* remind yourself to use particular lessons or books again next year and where to find those materials ("Borrowed from Ms. Smith").

Components of Curriculum Binders

A completed curriculum binder contains:

* a yearly overview of units of study you plan to carry out in reading or writing workshop.

* a tabbed section for each unit of study (which generally takes about a month) with an overview sheet listing your activities and goals for the unit. Each section contains materials lists, sample focus lessons, overhead transparencies of children's work for teaching, reproducible assessment tools, and articles and chapters from professional books that relate to the unit.

* general sections for reproducible assessment and organizational tools, a materials wish list, overview sheets, bibliographies, and anything else you feel you may need.

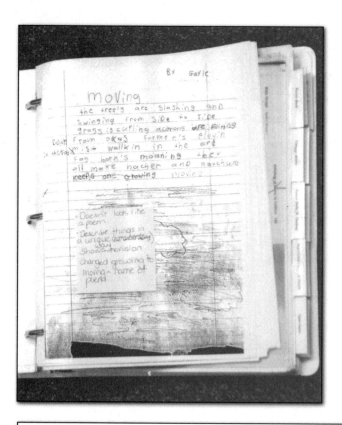

Yearly Overview Map

	STRATEGY FOCUS/READING	WRITING FOCUS
September	*Sense of Self as Reader* assessment/management "community of readers" What are good readers? building stamina basic monitoring book choice	*... as Writer* assessment/management "community of writers" ... good writers? building stamina basic editing filling the notebook
October	*Monitoring for Understanding* Begin partnerships/grouping for guided reading	*Gathering Information and Drafting* Do notebook process together.
November	*Making Connections* 3 ways of connecting/coding text; text to self, text to text; text to world written response	*Memoir* Begin using notebooks independently.
December/ January	*Questioning* responding to my questioning critical reading	*Writing for an Audience: Revision* genre: letter writing
January/ February	*Visualizing/Inferring* show, not tell elaboration and detail genre: poetry	*Writing with Clarity* show, not tell
February/ March	*Determining Importance* main idea and theme story mapping character mapping	*Narrative Focus in Notebooks* author's craft
April	*Determining Importance*	*Nonfiction Writing*
May	*Synthesis*	*Notebook Use Revisited*
June	*Sense of Self as Reader* considering identities and goals reflecting on growth planning for summer reading	*... as Writer* considering identities and goals reflecting on growth planning for summer writing

Elements of a completed curriculum binder

Writing Unit Overview

Topic/Unit of Study: *Memoir*   **Publication Date:** *10/25*

Type of Publication/Celebration: *typed-up book/parents invited for celebration*

Focus Lessons:
- Immersion in and collection of memoir
- What is memoir? memory vs. memoir (What does this say about who I am today?)
- Getting the memories into the room
- Memories are contained in photos and artifacts
- Envisioning end product, awareness of audience
- Craft of a picture book
- Time, chronological, and other retellings
- Zooming in, tiny details to paint a picture or develop a character
- Personal time lines (integrate with computers.)
- Narration, who is telling the story

Materials:
Usual writing workshop materials
Drafting folders
Small notebooks just for memoir

Read Alouds:
Owl Moon, J. Yolen
Cynthia Rylant
Jamie Lee Curtis
The House on Mango Street
Now One Foot, Now the Other, T.DePaola
See Memoir Box in language arts room
See Reading List in curriculum binder

Home/School: (homework)
Timeline, picture and artifacts
Stories from home, traditions

Assessment: Using rubric to compare first entry with developed piece/story. (Create rubric with students.)

Reflection:

Making Connections to Text
Sample Focus Lessons, Denise Bozutto, CT Regional District 6

Focus Lesson: Making Connections—reminders
(using background knowledge when reading)
Read Aloud: *Koala Lou*
Teacher uses think-aloud about connection she/he is making that reminds her/him of something. On a Post-it marked "R," teacher writes a few words about the connection to mark the spot in the text. (Post-it sticks out of book.)
Student Work:
During Read Aloud—During the last few pages of the text, students "say something" to their Read Aloud partner that reminds them of something. Teacher records on chart connection categories: text to self, text to text, text to world. Teacher may also have students do a 'public try' of the strategy in the rug area (i.e. each student reads for 3 minutes and recording a Post-it).
During independent reading—Students use three to four Post-its to record a few words to describe connections. During last five minutes of independent reading, students pair-share with a partner, discussing their Post-its.
During share—Teacher fishbowls a partnership with model responses or selects two or three students to share a Post-it. Teacher reviews objective: "Why is it important to think about what the text reminds you of?" and "Why is it important for your reading?"
Homework: Students reread today's pages and complete one more

Focus Lesson: Making Connections—reminders
(written response to text)
Read Aloud: *The Relatives Came* by Cynthia Rylant
On large chart paper, teacher models using a double-entry journal, using yesterday's Post-its. Teacher thinks aloud the process.
Student Work:
During Read Aloud—Students "say something" to their Read Aloud partner that could be written for last few Post-its. Teacher records responses.
During Independent Read—Students continue coding their text with R and a few words. During last ten minutes of independent reading, students record in double-entry journals and share with a partner.
During share—Two to three students share model entries. Teacher reviews why it is important to make text-to-self connections when reading.
Homework: Reread pages you have read today and complete another double-entry journal entry.

As valuable as the completed curriculum binder is, though, it's the process of creating it that helps us most because we must think about *why* we do certain things in our classrooms and not just what we do next.

Getting Started

Decide who will work on this project. Will you work on creating a curriculum binder on your own, using this book as your "colleague," with a partner, or with a group of teachers?

Hold weekly or biweekly meetings. Planning takes time, so allow for it. I recently heard a radio commercial that said, "time can mean the difference between a squashed grape and a fine wine." It's best if you can schedule several meetings in advance and mark your calendars in ink.

Some teachers designate every other grade-level meeting to the project. Others schedule before- or after-school meetings. You may be able to get together over lunch once a week. Is there a way to get release time to work on this project?

Limit the number of meetings. It's easier to commit to, say, six weeks of after-school meetings than to the entire school year. It's also easier to find release-time coverage if there is a finite number of meetings. If you want to continue meeting after the first six weeks, great. But limiting the number of meetings gives people an "out" if they feel they need it by the end.

Plan on spreading your work over several months. Don't try to do the project all at once. Instead, identify a target date to get everything done and map out a long-term plan. See if you can make the project part of a district-supported staff development initiative. I've worked with teachers who made the project part of their teacher evaluation process. Others collected continuing education credits from their state.

Decide on your focus. Will you begin by focusing on a reading or a writing curriculum? Reading and writing don't stand alone, and what you focus on in one will certainly overlap with the other. However, I find it is more productive and manageable to think of separate workshops when planning for the year. Starting with writing usually works best, especially among teachers without much workshop teaching experience. Once you have established a writing workshop, you can transfer the approach to reading.

Next Steps

After you have set aside time and decided on a focus for this project, take the following actions.

Purchase binders and dividers. You'll need two three-ring binders and tabbed divider pages. A three-hole punch will be handy, too. Threading binders are great because they enable you to add and remove material continually. I use the large three-inch size. They're large enough to hold everything you need, yet small enough to transport.

Read and start discussing professional materials. Take time to review the latest research on current best practices. I've already recommended the New Standards. There are several other great books listed at the end of Chapter 2. Give yourself reading assignments, take notes, and discuss the reading with your group. Keep a reading journal if you are working alone. Review and reflect on what you've learned from the first two chapters of this book. Find notes from professional development sessions you've attended recently. Reread them. Make copies of the bibliographies and charts. Take notes during discussions with colleagues. You'll be able to add them to your binders.

Start collecting articles and notes in your binders. Don't worry too much about organizing materials yet. You'll be fine-tuning as you go. To start, just keep materials related to writing in one binder and materials related to reading in the other. Some teachers have found it helpful to keep everything in a basket, which is handy to take to and from meetings. The finished curriculum binder will be a reflection of your growth as a literacy practitioner. Ideally, though, it won't ever be really finished. It should be a living document that's changing and growing all the time.

Clean out your files. Just like housecleaning or redecorating, get rid of anything you haven't used recently. However, add "treasures" you find to your binders. I went through my files recently. I got rid of material that no longer matched my understanding of literacy teaching. In order to know what to keep, I needed to be up on current professional materials, which is why I ask you to read those materials yourselves.

As you continue reading this book, make photocopies of charts, forms, lists, and anything else that you feel may be useful. Keep them in your binders as well. Again, don't worry too much about organizing them yet. As you begin to define your curriculum, it will become clear where to slot the materials so they will be most useful and accessible to you.

Planning Reading and Writing Workshops: Mapping Out Units of Study

Now we're going to take a closer look at units of study for reading and writing workshops and how they help us to organize and plan.

Units of Study in a Writing Workshop

As I mentioned earlier, units of study are periods of focus on a particular genre or strategy. In a writing workshop, for example, students might spend time studying poetry, memoir, or craft as a whole class, while working on individual projects. In a reading workshop, the focus might be on the use of a strategy, such as monitoring for meaning. Generally, deciding on what to do isn't the hard part. It's deciding when to end the unit and move on to another one that's difficult. That's where mapping out the year can help.

Teachers with whom I've worked have found the words of Isoke Nia of the Teachers College Reading and Writing Project at Columbia University to be infinitely wise when it comes to planning curriculum. Her article titled "Units of Study in the Writing Workshop" from the August 1999 issue of *Primary Voices*, which appears on pages 75–83, offers suggestions for planning units of study in writing workshops. They can be applied to planning units for reading workshop, too. Isoke explains, clearly and compellingly, the cycle of a unit of study. (In primary classrooms, units generally last about three to eight weeks.) She also provides helpful tips for choosing "touchstone texts," texts you can teach from and will return to again and again.

As you read Isoke's article, you'll notice that her focus is always on teaching the writers, even when immersed in a unit of study. She makes it quite clear that there's more to teaching writing than giving students a pattern with which to write narratives. It's about exposing them to a wide variety of genres and helping them to become independent.

Imagine how you might use her tips for planning units of study in your own workshops.

UNITS OF STUDY IN THE WRITING WORKSHOP

In writing workshops across the world, teachers are struggling with the repetitiveness of teaching the writing process. On their walls, they have charts that show the steps of the process in linear or circular shapes. They march their students progressively through these steps, time and time again, like a machine. Faced with the quandary, "What am I to teach?" in the seemingly endless cycle, they reluctantly answer, "I guess I teach how to do each of these steps better one more time or teach random mini-lessons on whatever comes up on a given day." As a study group, we wanted a better answer than that to this curriculum question, and so we searched together for an organizing structure for our writing workshops. We wanted to plan units of study that would carry us across the year with our students.

A unit of study in writing is not unlike a unit of study in science or social studies. It is a line of inquiry—a road of curriculum, a trail of teaching, an excursion of knowing something about writing. It is some big thing that you and your class are digging into over time. For several weeks you plan mini-lessons and lines of inquiry that allow your students to become actively involved in creating the curriculum around the unit of study. If some outside force is requiring you to study something—say, "personal narrative" for the fourth-grade writing test—you turn that requirement into a unit of study on memoir that actively involves students as real writers engaged in inquiry.

Planning the Year

School years are made of time, and so when we started we looked for ways we might wrap these inquiries around the approximately 180 days of our school year. We imagined the school calendar in increments of time, each lasting approximately three to eight weeks. Next, we had to think about what we might study. As we thought about our teaching and our experiences in writing workshop, we decided there were many possibilities for studies that might help our students grow as writers. We generated the following list of possibilities for units of study:

- genre studies: fiction, memoir,

Isoke Titilayo Nia

Director of Research and Development, The Reading and Writing Project, Teacher College, Columbia University, New York

poetry, essay, etc.

- the writing process itself, from idea to publication
- individual parts of the process, such as revision, editing, or gathering in the writing notebook
- living the writerly life
- collaboration (writing in partnerships and other groupings)
- a particular author
- the craft of writing: genre, structure, sound, language system
- difficulty—what are students struggling with?
- using a writer's notebook throughout the process
- stamina in the writing workshop (helping students develop muscles to make writing better)

Teachers must decide how much they want to prepare their students.

This list helped us envision what a whole year's worth of study might include. Each of us began the process of making important curricular decisions about what units we would include in our planning for the year and where we would place these units on the timeline of our study.

We first considered units of genre studies. The focus of a genre study is on a particular type of writing and its attributes. We began with genre study because it was what we thought we knew (though we would find out we had a lot to learn as we went along). Genre studies seemed available. We had read about them in our mentor books on the teaching of writing by

Randy Bomer (1995), Jo Ann Hindley (1996), and Lucy Calkins (1994), who wrote, "We regard genre studies as fundamental enough to shape our curriculum around them. We find that when an entire class inquires into a genre, it is life-giving" (p. 363). We remembered writing poems and stories as children, and, as avid readers, we knew lots of texts in different genres. So genre studies seemed a logical place to start and they seemed like units of study that could sustain us for much of the year.

Organizing for Genre Study

We learned through experience that regardless of the type of genre study we were having, the organization of the study was very similar. We organized a study of poetry in much the same way as we organized a study of fiction. The content was different, but the structure of the study was basically the same, as shown in the following structural frame for a genre study.

Genre Study Steps
Best-Guess Gathering
Immersion
Sifting
Second Immersion
Selecting Touchstone Texts
Touchstone Try-Its
Writing
Reflecting/Assessing

Best-Guess Gathering

When I get an image of what best-guess gathering looks like in a classroom, I am reminded of the treasure hunts that I participated in at the Brooklyn Museum as a child. I remember getting a clipboard and a short yellow pencil and then being let loose to find a list of treasures. I remember some children lagging behind because the clues on the clipboard didn't seem to be enough, and sometimes the instructors would say more about each clue before they sent us off. But most times it was just us and the clues. It wasn't like the instructors thought the clues were really all we had to go on. They knew we knew more. We were museum students. We were junior members of the museum and were expected to know something about it. Our monthly treasure hunts gave us a sense of ownership, a sense of "this is our museum." When I found the treasure, the museum was mine.

In best-guess gathering, the teacher and the students go into their world on a treasure hunt and bring to the classroom what they think are examples of the genre. Teachers must decide how much they want to say to prepare their students for the hunt. Many teachers do not define the genre at all, choosing instead to allow the definition of the genre to emerge from the gathered texts. They trust that students have in their minds an image of the genre and they want them to use this image to truly make a best guess. Other teachers might choose to say more—to give their students an image of the genre before they go out to gather. In the three genre studies in this issue, you will notice how each teacher makes this decision in her own way.

While most teachers invite their students in on the gathering, this part of the study can be as individual as a single teacher and an evening in the library. It can also be as large as announcements over the loudspeaker to an entire school population: "Class 2-499 is studying poetry. Please help them with their study by placing your favorite poem in the envelope outside their classroom door!" No matter how teachers choose to approach this step, they should wind up with a huge pile of "stuff"—of best-guess genre examples—that have been gathered.

Immersion

As the material comes into the room, the teacher and students are reading it together, immersing themselves in all their best-guess "stuff." As they choose interesting examples to read, they are beginning to pay attention to the sound and look of the genre and noticing the writing they admire. They are sorting the stuff into piles— categorizing in ways that help them define the genre. I have often asked students at this stage of a genre study to put things in piles that help them say smart things about the genre. I have to trust them to do this. I have to trust that everything they say is important and will somehow push the learning forward.

Around all the sorting and reading there must be a lot of talking. The students will use their talk to create a working definition of the genre as they notice generalities across examples. They will also notice so much more than they would if the definition of the genre had been handed to them in the beginning.

Students will notice so much more than they would if the definition of the genre had been handed to them in the beginning.

Sifting

After students have had time (three to four days) to look closely at the pieces of writing, they are ready to begin sifting. This is a process of selecting specific texts that will carry the genre study forward. We usually sift texts out for three reasons:

1. The text is not an example of the genre.

2. The text is an example of the genre, but it is not like what we will write. Because of such variety within genres, we must make a decision about what kinds of texts we will write. We keep only these kinds in our sifting.

3. The text belongs to the genre, and it is like what we will write, but it just isn't good writing. We just don't like it so we take it out. This is also when I'd remove anything that might not be appropriate content for the class to use as a model.

As you are sifting, remember that the world of literature is large. There is no reason for a single piece of literature that is not the best to be included in the study.

Second Immersion

Again the students need to immerse themselves in the genre, but this time they are looking at pieces that are exactly like the kind of writing they will be doing. This immersion has so much to do with the ears, with getting the sound of the genre inside the students. It is when students begin to look at the details of the pieces of writing. The beautiful beginnings and endings. The pictures that make you want to cry. During this immersion the teacher is looking for a touchstone text for the class, and the students are looking for mentor pieces for themselves. How do they know when they find them? When a piece seems to jump out of someone's small pile and literally scream his or her name followed by the names of all the students in the class, then that student or teacher has selected a touchstone text (see Figure 1).

Touchstone Try-Its

The touchstone text for the class is made available for every student. For several days students will read and talk about the text, discussing anything they notice about the writing. The focus of the inquiry at this point is to try to figure out how

Selecting Touchstone Texts

You have read the text and you love it.

"You" means the teacher! You love this text so much that you think just by reading it your students will fall instantly in love with it. Your love will be contagious.

You and your students have talked about the text a lot as readers first.

No piece of literature was written to be taken apart or dissected. It was written to speak to us and to help us change the lives we lead. Our first response to a piece of literature should be as readers. Talk first and talk well before you begin to dissect any piece of writing for your study.

You find many things to teach in the text.

The text feels full—teaching full. You see so much that you can teach using just this one piece of literature.

You can imagine talking about the text for a very long time.

Make sure that the text you choose can carry the weight of constant talk and examination.

Your entire class can have access to the text.

A touchstone no one can touch won't work. The piece you choose must be short enough to be put on overhead, make photocopies from, or have multiple copies of the book for no more than five or six students to share at a time.

Your students can read the text independently or with some support.

Because you are going to invest so much time and talk in this one piece of literature, you don't really need to worry about whether every child can read the text independently. This text is going to come with lots of support.

The text is a little more sophisticated than the writing of your best students.

You want every child to have to work to write like this author. Make sure you choose something that will be challenging. Trust the literature and study time to help students meet this challenge.

The text is written by a writer you trust.

When your back is up against a wall, have some old standbys to reach for. Have a few authors you know "by heart" and whose work you really trust.

The text is a good example of writing of a particular kind (genre).

There are some pieces of writing that are almost textbook examples of the genre. Look for these and save them *forever* because they so well represent what the genre is all about.

The text is of the genre that we are studying.

For first-time genre studies, try to keep the genre "pure"—meaning if you are studying memoir for the first time, you might not include memoir in the form of poetry or song. You might look only at narrative memoir that first time.

You have read the text and loved it.

And just in case you forgot, you have read it and fallen so deeply in love with this piece of writing that you feel privileged to use it in teaching. You run into your mini-lessons with joy because you have under your arm one of your favorites. Your love of the text is fuel for your study.

Figure 1. Characteristics of touchstone texts

the writer went about the writing. Students discuss decisions they think the writers of touchstone texts have made about such things as what to include in plot, or whether to repeat a word for effect, or which punctuation to use. The purpose of this close study and the conversations around it is to help students envision new possibilities for their own writing.

In mini-lessons and conferences, the teacher is asking students to "try it," try out the different writing moves they have noticed professional authors using. The touchstone try-it is safe, even playful. Students try things in notebooks and drafts just to see how they sound. If they like some writing a touchstone author has helped them to do, they may include what they have tried in their actual publications. The try-its especially help students who are reluctant to revise, giving them a range of options to explore during revision. During a conference, a teacher might help a student try a writing move out loud so the student can hear how the writing would sound. The teacher is alert for places in notebooks and drafts where it might make sense to suggest try-its to students.

Writing

Students *write* throughout the genre study. They are collecting entries in their notebooks, nurturing seed ideas for projects, playing with touchstone try-its, publishing pieces for their own reasons, and so on. In the step-by-step structural frame for genre study that I outlined above, the writing step refers to the drafting, revising, and editing of a published piece in the genre under study. The writing time for this is fairly short (usually about six days) because of all the genre study work that has come before it. There is an additional time period for the actual publishing of this piece of work if it is to be presented in a particular way, such as in a class magazine or in an anthology of poetry.

Reflecting/Assessing

After any study (genre or otherwise)

the teacher and students should spend some time reflecting on and assessing their work. They should look at both their processes and their products. This assessment can be as simple as a narrative—having students answer a question, or several questions, about their work:

- How did going through this study feel?
- What was hard for you?
- What do you think about your finished piece?

Assessment may also be as demanding as a rubric created jointly by teacher and students. The assessment tool that you choose should reflect the sophistication of your students. I try to begin the year with the narrative question assessment, then move to checklists and rubrics, and end my year with a combination of both. Whichever tool you use should always lead to more talk among you and your students. Your goal is not just to have students complete writing projects. You want them to really understand these projects, and you want to use their understandings to revise your teaching.

The beauty of this frame for a genre study is that it can be used to organize so much good teaching in the writing workshop. The driving force behind this kind of study is the principle of immersion, the idea that students and teachers need to be deep readers of whatever kind of

Whichever assessment tool you use should always lead to more talk among you and your students.

writing they are learning to do. And equally beautiful is the fact that you can be a learner alongside your students. Beginning a study means trusting the learner part of you. You don't need to know everything there is to know about a genre to do a genre study with your students. It is good to have some background knowledge—which you can acquire by reading examples of the genre, books by writers about writing, and books on the teaching of writing—but the best knowledge comes from active involvement in the study with your class.

Benefits of Study in the Classroom

Units of study are essential to the writing workshop because without them, what is the work of the workshop on a day-to-day basis? Like a learning map you and your students chart together, your studies create a year's worth of curriculum for the workshop that exposes students to new possibilities as writers.

Units of study help to set the pace for your workshop. They add quality and consistency that both students and teachers need in a workshop setting. When study is valued and arranged with skill and care in a school year, a teacher can both expose her students to many genres and have them become

experts in a few. When units of study are planned around writing issues other than genre, students are exposed to a wide range of helpful curriculum for their writing lives. Smaller studies (mini-inquiries) of one week or so can be carefully placed between longer studies when they are necessary to meet student needs. These small studies create a sense of continuity in the work.

Many teachers have found it useful to develop a calendar for units of study during the year. One example is presented in the Classroom Connections at the end of this essay. Notice the units selected and the length of time allotted for each.

This calendar becomes public knowledge. It is the learning map that we and our students will use. Publication dates are spread out liberally across the calendar to insure that we will publish often and to give us something to live toward in our studies. This is the quality that we strive for in our work together: planfulness. It is something like how we live our social lives. We plan a social calendar with specific dates and occasions, but we always make sure we leave room for the unexpected—the last-minute tickets to a great play or the dinner invitation to the new restaurant in town.

Teachers have to think of curriculum calendars in much the same way: We learned that we cannot

Sharing with our students this sort of "calendar approach" to planning for the writing workshop has raised both the production level and the quality of students' writing.

map out the whole year in August. We learned that to live towards study meant we had to plan several times a year. We had to look at our calendars and our students often and reshape our plans. We learned to trust our August thinking and our November thinking and to let one nourish the other. A part of that learning was to accept that we couldn't really know what our whole calendar would look like until we got to June. It wasn't that we weren't thinking about June much earlier in the year. We just realized that we had to remain open to the possibilities that June might bring.

We also learned to take time (in August and at several points during the school year) to follow these lines of thinking:

- Can I imagine how I'd like the work to go?

- What would I like my students to get from a study?

- Why am I tackling this hard work?

- Can I imagine a time span?

- What are the structures I need to exist in my classroom to make this type of learning possible? How can we get them in?

- How important are the writing notebooks going to be?

- What supplies and literature need to exist in this classroom to make our work possible, and where or how are we going to acquire them?

- What lessons will I need to teach? (Leave room for some you can't imagine yet. Pay close attention to what is happening in your class. Take good notes. Study your conferences. THEN, ask yourself again, "What lessons will I need to teach?")

- With whom will I share this learning journey? (Don't travel alone. It's easier with a friend by your side.)

We reflected on these questions periodically as a group and as individuals. They helped us know what needed to come next on our planful journey through the curriculum year.

Raising the Level of Work

We have found that sharing with our students this sort of "calendar approach" to planning for the writing workshop—setting publication dates and making clear what will be studied—has raised both the production level and the quality of writing our students produce. The predictable immersion part of any study of writing helps students learn to read like writers. Over time, reading like writers through thoughtful, well-planned units of study helps students develop an excellent sense of what good writing is so that they can identify and emulate it wherever they find it in the world.

Units of study in the writing workshop also allow students to discover the kinds of writers they are. The child that loves poetry will shine during the poetry study and cringe (perhaps) during the nonfiction genre study but will have many spaces in between to write in the genre that she or he wishes. The beauty of genre study is that it never removes a child's right to choose a topic. Though students may gather to study a very particular kind of writing, they are always writing about topics they have chosen themselves. The studies strengthen their sense of craft and help them envision all the possibilities that exist for their ideas.

Note

All of the writers included in this issue are members of a Writing Leadership Group within The Teachers College Reading and Writing Project, Columbia University, Leadership Project. This group is led by Isoke Titilayo Nia and funded by a grant written by the projects director, Lucy Calkins, from Morgan Guaranty Trust Company of New York.

References

Bomer, R. (1995). *Time for Meaning: Crafting Literate lives in Middle and High School.* Portsmouth, NH: Heinemann.

Calkins, L. (1994). *The Art of Teaching Writing.* Portsmouth, NH: Heinemann.

Hindley, J. (1996). *In the Company of Children.* York, ME: Stenhouse.

Units of Study in a Reading Workshop

Isoke's article helps us think about possibilities for studies that help our students grow as writers. But how do her ideas translate into units of study for the reading workshop? The teachers with whom I have worked have found several sources for answers to that question. We begin with the proficient reader research by Pearce et al. (1992). Proficient readers

* search for connections between what they know and the new information they encounter in the texts they read.

* ask questions of themselves, authors, and the texts they read.

* draw inferences during and after reading.

* distinguish important from less important ideas in text.

* are adept at synthesizing information within and across texts and reading experiences.

* repair faulty comprehension.

* monitor the adequacy of their understanding.

I would add

* visualize and create images using the different senses to better understand what they read (Keene and Zimmerman, 1997).

Tips for Strategy Instruction

According to Stephanie Harvey and Anne Goudvis, authors of *Strategies That Work*, teaching students to read strategically means we show them how to construct meaning when they read. Comprehension strategy instruction is most effective when teachers:

◆ model their use of the strategy repeatedly over time.

◆ show students their thinking when reading, and articulate how that thinking helps them better understand what they read.

◆ discuss how the strategy helps readers make meaning.

◆ make connections between the new strategy and what the reader already knows.

◆ respond in writing by coding the text according to a particular strategy (once kids are reading on their own).

Possible Topics for Units of Study

The next section describes some possible units of study for reading
workshop. I've clustered the units into two categories: *Habits of Good
Readers* and *Strategies of Good Readers*.

Habits of Good Readers

Thinking of Ourselves as Readers

Do our students consider themselves readers even if they haven't yet
begun to "crack the code"? Do we consider them readers? It's important
to build their identities as readers early on. What types of focus lessons
can you envision that would support readers' identity?

> We're the kind of readers who...
>
> like to get books for presents.
>
> read every day.
>
> like to read books in a series.
>
> enjoy mysteries (or animal books or
> <u>Frog and Toad</u>).
>
> like to talk about books.

**This chart was created by primary students while discussing
who they are as readers.**

Planning Our Reading Lives

We can show students that good readers plan their reading lives and
have goals for themselves as readers. During a unit of study, focus
lessons can cover "planfulness." You might ask students to share their
plans for the next reading session, during the focus lesson or share time.
("I plan on finishing this book," or "I plan on finding other books by this

author.") You might also ask students to choose books for future reading. Michele Masi, a first-grade teacher, has her students recommend books to each other.

Choosing Books That Are Just Right for Us

Can our students choose books that are "just right" for them? What does a "just right" book feel like? I used to tell my first graders that finding a just right book would help them grow as readers by allowing them to use their "reading muscles." I would compare the selection process to riding a bike: "If you choose a book that's too hard, it might be like riding up a steep hill. Sure, you'd be using your muscles, but you probably would also be straining so hard that you wouldn't notice any of the scenery. If you always choose a book that's too easy, it's like coasting down the hill. You don't use your muscles, so you're not growing as a reader. Plus, you're going too fast to enjoy the scenery. A 'just right' book is like a 'just right' bike ride with some small hills. It allows you to exercise your reading muscles while enjoying the scenery." Spend some time thinking about how you can support independent book choice in your room. Think leveled library.

Book choice also involves knowing the type of reader you are and which types of books you like. That's where book orientation comes in. It deals with what good readers do *before* they start reading. Good readers usually flip through the book, maybe looking at pictures. They might think about other books they've read by the author, or other books on the same topic. Good readers usually begin reading with some questions in mind.

Talking About Books We Read

Independent reading is rarely "independent." Reading can be a social activity. Even mature readers have dialogues before, during, and after reading. When I finish reading a book, for example, I'll often pass it along to my mother or sister-in-law. I love to talk about a good book with someone else who has read it. Even when I'm reading a book I don't want to share, I have a "conversation" with the characters ("Don't open that door!") or with the author ("Now, how could you kill off that character?").

We want students to know that good readers instinctively talk about books to develop ideas and meaning. We want them to share and talk about books with each other in natural ways. We want them to notice the kinds of talking about books they may already be doing.

How do we make this happen for our youngest readers in a unit of study? We can invite mature readers into the class to be interviewed about their social reading habits. We can ask our students to interview someone at home. We can model our own social reading lives: "I just finished a book that my sister gave me. I called her last night and we talked for an hour about it. Don't you just love to talk about books with friends? What can we do in our classroom to make it easier to talk about our reading?" I'm always surprised by the answers even our youngest readers give.

Encourage discussion outside of the classroom, too. My daughter recently formed a summer reading book club. She and her friends read the same book and then get together in her tree house to discuss it. They have discovered that it's helpful to mark interesting pages with sticky notes to facilitate their talks. And it works—their book discussions last a long time. Good readers love to talk about books.

Reading Across Genres and Text Types

Good readers use strategies flexibly, across different genres and kinds of texts. For a unit of study, you might include:

* poetry
* ABC books
* list books
* "old favorites"
* mysteries
* fiction
* fantasy
* book reviews
* signs

* songs
* newspapers, magazines
* directions to games
* TV listings
* comic strips
* jokes and riddles
* charts and graphs
* maps
* schedules

Focus on how the use of strategies changes depending on what you are reading.

Strategies of Good Readers

Monitoring for Understanding

Do our students recognize when what they are reading doesn't make sense? Are they reading with an ear towards understanding, making sure it "sounds right"—or are they simply word calling, what I call "mechanical reading"? We want students to listen as they read to make sure what they say makes sense, grammatically and semantically. Students need to be consistently monitoring for understanding before they can successfully apply certain higher-level strategies.

We can make sure they understand this concept by modeling during read alouds and shared reading, by conferring with students during guided reading and independent reading, and by sharing the process of monitoring for meaning during share time of reading workshop. By listening to students read and then asking, "Does that sound right to you?" or "What would make sense there?" we offer support without becoming a crutch. Eventually our young readers will ask themselves these questions on their own.

Using Strategies to Figure Out Words

To figure out unfamiliar words, good readers use initial consonants and look through to the end of the word. Other strategies they use—and you could teach in a unit of study—include chunking, using picture clues, thinking about what would make sense, integrating strategy use, and focusing on prefixes and suffixes.

Making Connections

By focusing on making connections, we ask beginning readers to do explicitly what mature readers do subconsciously. Harvey and Goudvis teach children to categorize and code their connections in order to be able to analyze and discuss them:

* **Text to self:** Does this text (story, song, poem, article, letter) relate to me?

* **Text to text:** Does this text relate to another text I know?

* **Text to world:** Does this text relate to something going on in the world?

They encourage students to share their connections in natural ways: "That reminds me of . . ." or "That's like the other story we read." (I was once in a kindergarten class, listening in on a conversation about Jane Yolen's *Owl Moon*. One student explained how the book reminded him of a time he and his grandmother went bird-watching, to which a classmate responded, "That's a text-to-grandma connection!")

Often teachers list on a chart the connections students make during a shared reading session. Then they analyze the connections as either "thick" or "thin." "Thick" connections support our understanding of the text: "I can understand how the character feels because I was new to this school this year," for example. However, a comment such as "White is my favorite color" about a passage in *Owl Moon* that describes snow is not as thick.

Questioning

Good readers ask questions before reading ("I wonder what this will be about?" "Why is the woman crying on the front cover?" "Who wrote this?"), during reading ("What is going to happen next?" "Why are the people so mean?" "Why did she leave?" "Huh? That doesn't make sense."), and after reading ("I wonder what would have happened if she had left earlier?" "How could it end that way?" "What else has this author written?").

Teachers can model questioning while thinking out loud during read alouds and shared reading, as well as during individual conferences. We chart questions while reading and later go back to see which have been answered. Answers to some questions can be found by rereading text. But some cannot. They must be inferred. I've found that the best questioning leads to inferential thinking.

Visualizing/Inferring

Creating pictures in our minds, or visualizing, helps us to understand what we are reading, fill in missing information, and build meaning. When we visualize, we combine the author's words with our own background knowledge.

When we infer, we use clues to draw conclusions about something that has happened or will happen. Inferences are different from predictions—predictions can be confirmed after reading, yet inferences generally can't. My friend and colleague, Lynn Holcomb, once said that she always thought of inferring as a third grade skill. It was, after all, listed in the third-grade curriculum where she taught. After spending the past several years working as a staff developer and college instructor, she's had to rethink her former beliefs. She has spent countless hours analyzing picture books and learned an important lesson related to inferring: In books like *Just Me and My Puppy* or *Henry and Mudge*, the pictures often tell a very different story than the words. If children aren't attending to the pictures, they will miss important points of the story. In *Just Me and My Puppy*, for example, the text tells how obedient and well trained the dog is, but the pictures tell an entirely different story, a very funny story. Many students miss that and don't realize it's supposed to be funny. Indeed, much of the story can be inferred from the pictures.

Determining Importance

Making meaning requires the reader to determine what is important. Readers have to decide what's relevant and ignore other kinds of information. This isn't learned by filling in worksheets. Readers who are given a chance to question and comment during reading begin to instinctively know what is important.

Synthesizing

Good readers think about what they read and stop every now and then to merge new information with their existing knowledge. In units of study, we can teach students to view the end of a page as a place to stop and think about what they are reading. Some of our beginning readers spend so much time trying to figure out the words, they forget to take time to digest the parts of their reading to construct meaning.

It is important to realize that we need to teach reading comprehension in the primary grades, along with decoding. These units of study are appropriate for readers at all levels because the strategies don't change; the level of reading material does. You could have a group of students working on the same strategy in a guided reading session, reading different books at different levels. Knowing what strategies your students are and are not using, and knowing book levels and how they support strategy is what its all about. I present a closer look at what a specific unit of study looks like in Chapters 5 and 6.

Your Plans Will Continue to Change and Grow

The first part of this book has been about *why* we should plan intentionally for literacy instruction. When I lead workshops for teachers, I often begin by asking what their "big questions" are about teaching reading and writing. I want to know what they hope to have answered by coming to the workshop. Doing so gives me a sense of who my audience is (i.e., using assessment to drive instruction) and helps me decide what information will meet participants' needs. It also gives the participants a sense of ownership. In the end, we always end up with more questions and implications for further study. In fact, leading a workshop reminds me of writing a dissertation. It's freeing to realize I don't have to come up with all the answers. The best workshops and dissertations end with questions for future study.

So, make your curriculum plans to the best of your ability today. The plans will change. You will grow. Your district mandates may change. Your administration may change. The students in your class will change this year and every year. A plan is always growing.

As I said so many times to my builder during my house renovation, "Might as well, while we're at it." I wouldn't have the great arched hallway in my dining room with the terrific view if I had stuck rigidly to the architect's original plan. He was the expert, but I live in my house. I see the view every day and I know my family and how we use our space. Yes, you may be told by the experts (for example, textbooks, teacher's manuals, or district mandates) what to do. But you are the one living in your classroom with your students.

I find this entry in the *Dictionary of Word Origins* interesting: "Plan: a flat representation on a flat surface. Etymologically—a design that has been "planted" on the ground. Originally referred to the laying out of the ground plan of a building."

Just as an architect's plan doesn't represent the life that happens within the building, your curriculum plan doesn't represent the life within your classroom, the joys and sorrows which take place within the community. The rooms' shapes, the decor, and the way the light comes in the window all have an effect on what goes on inside a house, just as a unit of study shapes what is going on in the classroom. It boils down to finding balance between the plan and the action, the day-to-day living.

As you plan your year and start to gain a sense of control over literacy teaching, remember to give yourself time. Also, the final document will never be truly finished. You can always revise and change it as you go. When we're intentional, we feel in control, and when we feel in control, we like what we're doing, and if we like what we're doing, we'll do it more, and the more we do it, the more intentional we'll be, and so it goes. . . .

Of course, it's our students who reap the benefits. If we are intentional in creating the best possible learning experiences for them, they will feel more in control of their reading and writing, which will cause them to like it more, and if they like it, they'll do more, and if they do more, they'll continue to grow, and, of course, the more they grow, the more they'll like it, and so it goes for them, too.

Stages in Planning Curriculum

1. Make time to plan. (Chapter 3)

2. Define "getting the job done" (vision, goals, and roles). (Chapters 1 and 2)

3. Map out the year of units of study in each workshop. (Chapter 4)

4. Plan each unit of study, keeping in mind workshop components. (Chapter 5)

5. Translate units of study into weekly and daily plans. (Chapter 6)

6. Reflect at the end of each unit, make changes, and plan ahead. (Chapter 7)

Part II
How to Plan

4

The Big Picture
Creating the Year-Long Plan

> *"One learns by doing a thing; for though you think you know it, you have no certainty until you try."*
> —Sophocles

Once you've defined your goals, started gathering materials, and given some thought to units of study, it's time to organize your curriculum and put together your binders. You'll start by mapping out the year in month-long units of study, made up of roughly ten months of school, ten units of study. (Be sure to account for the fact that some units will take less than a month to complete, while others may take slightly longer.) Get your binders ready by creating a section and tab for each unit. Other sections to consider:

* Overview Sheets
* Spelling/Word Work Materials
* Assessment/Conferring Tools

* Supplies/Books Wish List
* Bibliographies
* Miscellaneous Blackline Masters

You may decide to start with your writing curriculum first, as the teachers at Roberts Avenue School and Stillmeadow School did. Or, like the teachers from Tracey School and the teachers from District 6 in Connecticut, you may decide to tackle reading first. I suggest gathering materials for both binders simultaneously, but focusing on organizing one to start.

Steps in Putting Together Your Curriculum Binder

The first step is to form a "big picture" plan for your year. What makes sense for your grade at the beginning of the school year, the middle, and the end? You may want to begin writing workshop by studying purposes for writing, the importance of creating community, and self-selecting writing topics. What kinds of school-wide events will you have to consider? The teachers at Stillmeadow School and Roberts Avenue School plan for Read Across America Day in the spring. When is National Poetry month? It's helpful to consider the school year in terms of ten months of three- to eight-week cycles.

But before deciding when to teach, you'll have to decide what to teach. Let's start with writing and move to reading later in the chapter.

In *The Writing Workshop: Working Through the Hard Parts (And They're All Hard Parts)*, Katie Wood Ray offers these questions to help us choose what to include in our writing curriculum:

* What are my strengths as a teacher of writing?

* What have my students studied before in writing?

* What are my students interested in? What do they want to know as writers?

* What are my colleagues studying in their writing workshops?

* What resources do I have?

* For what kind of writing will my students be held accountable?

What unit-of-study topics in writing do you imagine doing with your students? Think in terms of genres (memoir, poetry, etc.) and topics like craft or revision. Create your list here.

_____

_____

_____

_____

_____

_____

_____

_____

After considering these and other questions, the teachers at Roberts Avenue School produced this list of topics to start with:

* sense of self as a writer

* topic choice

* poetry

* memoir

* getting writing on the page

* revision

Other topics to consider:

* nonfiction

* craft (such as descriptive language, or parts of story)

* editing

* author study

* writing partners

* reading and rereading our writing

Use the Yearly Overview Map on page 98 to begin mapping out your curriculum. Once you have a list of topics, decide when to teach each unit. You will need your official school calendar to plan for the year. What will be the focus for the beginning of the year? Do you and your colleagues plan on doing any units together?

It makes sense to study certain topics at certain times of the year. For instance, a good unit for the beginning of the year might focus on building a community of readers and/or writers where students write, by themselves and in a group, about their reading and writing lives. You'll probably want to leave open some spaces in the year, too. Don't forget to consult your district's curriculum document and your school's official calendar. When are vacations? Professional development days? Standardized tests? School-wide special events?

It's always smart to tie these events into your curriculum somehow, if it seems natural to do so. For example, for Read Across America Day, the students at Stillmeadow School had a school-wide author celebration. Prior to the event, each child was given a blank book and was expected to have a completed project in time for the celebration. Teachers decided what they would be studying in February, with an eye toward that project. Some classes filled their blank books by writing memoirs. Some of the younger students wrote concept books, after studying many·published examples. Some children wrote poetry anthologies.

To Do: Brainstorm the year. Refer back to the New Standards description on page 44 and the work you did in the beginning chapters of this book. What have you decided are the most important concepts to study? Is what you are planning part of accepted current best practice? In the next chapter, we'll take a closer look at each month and begin to translate this big-picture overview into usable plans for each unit.

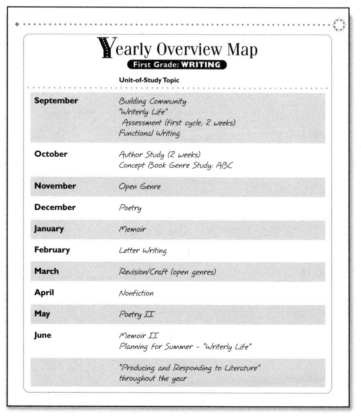

Yearly Overview Map
First Grade: WRITING
Unit-of-Study Topic

Month	Unit-of-Study Topic
September	Building Community "Writerly Life" Assessment (first cycle, 2 weeks) Functional Writing
October	Author Study (2 weeks) Concept Book Genre Study: ABC
November	Open Genre
December	Poetry
January	Memoir
February	Letter Writing
March	Revision/Craft (open genres)
April	Nonfiction
May	Poetry II
June	Memoir II Planning for Summer - "Writerly Life"
	"Producing and Responding to Literature" throughout the year

The plan that the first-grade teachers at Roberts Avenue School developed.

Yearly Overview Map
WRITING

Unit-of-Study Topic

August
_____
_____
_____

September _____
_____
_____

October _____
_____
_____

November _____
_____
_____

December _____
_____
_____

January _____
_____
_____

February _____
_____
_____

March _____
_____
_____

April _____
_____
_____

May _____
_____
_____

June _____
_____
_____

There were specific reasons for some of the choices the teachers made. Their district curriculum calls for studying a variety of genres and for "producing and responding to literature," so they decided to cover those topics throughout the year. The year before they created this plan, I worked with them on a poetry unit of study. Specifically, we studied teaching poetry while looking at writing workshop in general. Students gave the poems they wrote as holiday gifts. The teachers liked the way the unit worked for them and decided to include poetry in their plan for the following year as well.

Other teachers like to start their year with poetry because the lessons students learn carry over into the rest of the workshop (for example, close observation to detail, writing with voice, beginning with a feeling, and an awareness of craft and revision). Also, we've found that writers who may not be successful at other forms of writing seem to shine during a poetry study. Other teachers prefer to introduce poetry later in the year, during National Poetry month in the spring. I know one school that has a school-wide poetry celebration in February. It makes sense for those classes to study poetry in January.

There is no wrong or right way to plan. When having conversations about best practices, we can decide if what we are doing is helping us be intentional in meeting the needs of our readers and writers.

Yearly Overview Map
Kindergarten: WRITING

Unit-of-Study Topic

Month	Topic
September	Writer's Life/Sense of Self as a Writer
October	Rereading Stretching Out Words/Spacing Word
November	Revision
December	Poetry
January	Picture Book Study (writing first, then drawing)
February	Introduction to a Variety of Genres
March	Open Genres
April	Editing
May	Memoir
June	Reflecting on growth as a writer (What can I do now that I couldn't do in September?)

A kindergarten writing plan may look something like this.

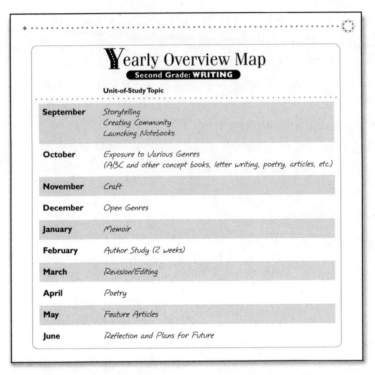

Yearly Overview Map

Second Grade: WRITING

Unit-of-Study Topic

September	Storytelling Creating Community Launching Notebooks
October	Exposure to Various Genres (ABC and other concept books, letter writing, poetry, articles, etc.)
November	Craft
December	Open Genres
January	Memoir
February	Author Study (2 weeks)
March	Revision/Editing
April	Poetry
May	Feature Articles
June	Reflection and Plans for Future

The second-grade teachers at Tracey School in Norwalk, Connecticut, developed this plan.

No two plans will look the same. However, there may be some overlap. Now, we'll take a look at plans for a reading curriculum.

Identifying and Scheduling Units for the Reading Curriculum

The following excerpt from Lucy Calkins' *The Art of Teaching Reading* reminds us of the need to broaden our definition of teaching reading.

When we plan for September in a primary reading workshop, we need to think in terms of what children need. Specifically, they need to:

◆ learn about when and why people read and write.

◆ develop concepts of school and of themselves as students. It is crucial for them to learn to be active, constructive, and engaged learners.

◆ develop concepts of language. It is fundamental for them to talk with each other and with us in sustained narratives.

◆ develop a concept of genre and to internalize a felt sense of the registers and structures of different genres so they can, for example, pick up a storybook and expect to find characters and a sequence of events. We hope the child will expect a recipe book to sound differently than a story.

◆ learn the concept of sound-letter correspondences.

◆ develop an understanding of words.

◆ develop print-specific directionality, to learn that most English writing is read from front to back, top to bottom, and left to right, unless the text has been arranged in a playful manner.

How do we design a curriculum that helps all our students come to school and feel smart and also gives them experience in working with print and stories that allows them to slowly consolidate the network of relationships involved in reading and writing? How, especially, do we teach big concepts—such as what different genres are like and why people read and write—when our children can't yet read conventionally?

—from Lucy McCormick Calkin's *The Art of Teaching Reading*, published by Allyn and Bacon, Boston, MA. © 2001 by Pearson Education. Adapted by permission of the publisher.

Think about the big ideas you might explore as a whole group in reading workshop. Again, you may want to refer back to the earlier chapters in this book and any additional research you may have done. You may want to consider the following:

✳ Sense of self as a reader/identity ("I'm the kind of reader who . . .")

✳ What it means to be a community of readers

✳ Choosing "just right" books and other reading materials

✳ Using strategies to figure out words/using all sources of information

✳ Monitoring for understanding/detecting errors

✳ Making connections (text-to-text, text-to-self, text-to-world)

* Revisiting text to support ideas

* Questioning authors and texts

* Visualizing and inferring as we read

* Determining what's important in what we read

* Synthesizing and interpreting what we read

What are the unit-of-study topics in reading you can imagine studying with your class?

_____

_____

_____

_____

_____

Now decide what you will focus on each month. On the next page, fill in the Yearly Overview Map for your reading curriculum.

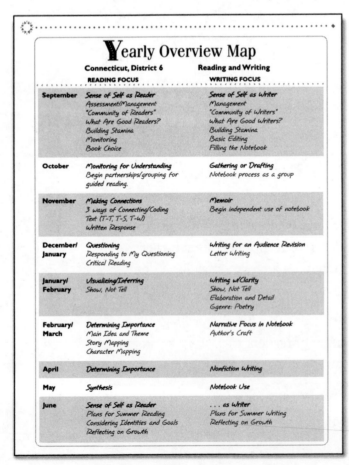

Yearly Overview Map

Connecticut, District 6   **Reading and Writing**

	READING FOCUS	WRITING FOCUS
September	*Sense of Self as Reader* *Assessment/Management* *"Community of Readers"* *What Are Good Readers?* *Building Stamina* *Monitoring* *Book Choice*	*Sense of Self as Writer* *Management* *"Community of Writers"* *What Are Good Writers?* *Building Stamina* *Basic Editing* *Filling the Notebook*
October	*Monitoring for Understanding* *Begin partnerships/grouping for guided reading.*	*Gathering or Drafting* *Notebook process as a group*
November	*Making Connections* *3 ways of Connecting/Coding Text (T-T, T-S, T-W)* *Written Response*	*Memoir* *Begin independent use of notebook*
December/ January	*Questioning* *Responding to My Questioning* *Critical Reading*	*Writing for an Audience Revision* *Letter Writing*
January/ February	*Visualizing/Inferring* *Show, Not Tell*	*Writing w/Clarity* *Show, Not Tell* *Elaboration and Detail* *Ggenre: Poetry*
February/ March	*Determining Importance* *Main Idea and Theme* *Story Mapping* *Character Mapping*	*Narrative Focus in Notebook* *Author's Craft*
April	*Determining Importance*	*Nonfiction Writing*
May	*Synthesis*	*Notebook Use*
June	*Sense of Self as Reader* *Plans for Summer Reading* *Considering Identities and Goals* *Reflecting on Growth*	*... as Writer* *Plans for Summer Writing* *Reflecting on Growth*

Denise Bozutto, language arts coordinator for District 6 in Connecticut, put together this map for reading and writing that includes strategies from Harvey and Goudvis's *Strategies That Work: Teaching Comprehension to Enhance Understanding*. Think of your grade level and what you would keep or change in Denise's plan.

Yearly Overview Map
READING

Unit-of-Study Topic

August

September

October

November

December

January

February

March

April

May

June

Yearly Overview Map

Kindergarten   **Reading and Writing**

	READING FOCUS	WRITING FOCUS
September	Good Habits Assessments Management/Routines Sense of Self as a Reader	Good Habits Topic Choice What Are Good Writers? Sense of Self as a Writer
October	Strategies for Figuring Out Words Reading Poetry	Storytelling Topic Choice, cont.
November/ December	Growing Ideas Through Talk	Poetry
January– May	Readers Follow Their Interests Multiple Options Strategies for Words II Building Stamina Character Studies	Writers Follow . . . Variety of Genres Author Study Craft Revision
May–June	Reflection/Planning	Reflection/Planning

A yearly map for kindergarten may look like this.

—adapted from work done by the Teachers College
Reading and Writing Project

Points to Consider When Marking Your Calendar

While planning your year, keep in mind student publication dates. You'll want to have at least 8 to 12 publication celebrations a year, which roughly translates to one per month. Usually when I tell teachers that, they groan. That's because we are accustomed to thinking about publication celebrations as full-blown tea parties, with parents and the public invited to see and hear typed-up, hardbound books created by our students. Those kinds of celebrations are nice, and I recommend them once or even twice a year, but certainly not ten times.

How you celebrate the end of a month-long poetry unit will probably look very different from how you celebrate a two-week unit on revision. Whereas you might do something grand for poetry, a unit on revision may end with a child simply sharing with classmates how he "fixed up" his piece. In kindergarten, a child may share how he added more details to his writing, in first grade, how he worked on his ending to make it more satisfying, and, in second grade, how he added dialogue to his piece and worked toward conventional spelling.

So use ink to mark your calendar for publication dates and don't worry too much about how the students publish. By setting up the dates beforehand, you'll structure your workshops. I remember conducting a memoir genre study with my first graders. Even though we had been studying memoir for five weeks, I just didn't feel they were ready to publish. I dragged the study on for a few more weeks and, really, we didn't get much further. I began to run out of ideas and so did the students. We all got bored. When I started setting dates for publication, though, we somehow managed to finish on time. I also learned to accept the fact that the work will never be perfect. We have to get what we can from each unit of study and move on.

Now that you have a yearly map in place, we turn to Chapter 5 to focus on turning that map into monthly plans. Then, in Chapter 6, we'll take a close look at how those monthly plans can be translated into daily plans.

To Do: You may decide to create your yearly maps in a group. That doesn't mean that everyone will plan the same units at the same time. There are reasons to align your curriculum plans with colleagues and reasons not to. Discuss the pros and cons, and come up with maps of your own.

A Closer Look

Creating Monthly Plans

> *"Education is not about filling a bucket, it is about lighting a fire."*
> —John Taylor Gatto

Now, here comes the fun part: translating those yearly overview maps into monthly plans. If you haven't done it already, create a tabbed divider page for each of your binder's month and/or unit sections, and then sort the materials you've collected so far. Use your divider pages to indicate what should go in each pile. Here's how one teacher labeled her tabbed sections:

Overview	Supplies/Wish List
Sept./"Writerly Life"	Spelling/Word Work
Oct./Functional Writing	Blackline Masters
Nov./Poetry	Bibliographies
Dec. through June . . .	Assessment/Conferring

Many teachers find it helpful to take everything they've collected out of their binders and sort it on a large table. The floor works well too! This alone could take up one of your scheduled study group meeting times. The yearly overview map, which you created in Chapter 4, should be one of the first pages in your binder, for easy reference. Some teachers use binders with clear plastic cover sleeves, which enables them to see the whole year at a glance.

You'll also be filling in a Unit-of-Study Overview Form for each section/month like the one shown below. Blank templates for writing and reading appear on pages 108 and 109. Photocopy enough templates for each unit you're planning and insert them into appropriate sections of your binder.

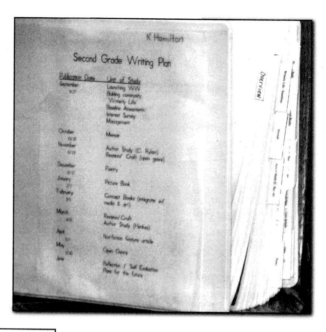

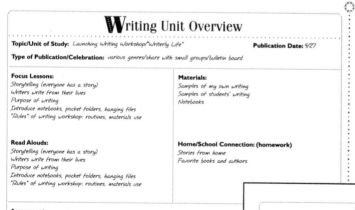

Sample completed Unit-of-Study Overview Forms for reading and writing.

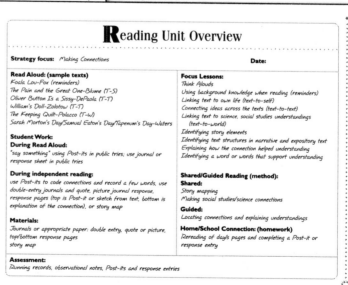

Writing Unit Overview

Topic/Unit of Study:

Type of Publication/Celebration:

Publication Date:

Focus Lessons:

Materials:

Read Alouds:

Home/School Connection: (homework)

Assessment:

Reflection:

Reading Unit Overview

Date:

Strategy focus:

Read Aloud: (sample texts)

Student Work:
During Read Aloud:

Focus Lessons:

During independent reading:

Shared/Guided Reading: (method)

Shared:

Guided:

Home/School Connection: (homework)

Materials:

Assessment:

Monthly Planning for Writing

To create plans that help us to be intentional, we need to consider all aspects of a good writing workshop. That way, we ensure that our focus lessons, materials, the type of publishing we do, and so forth support our units of study. Teachers who plan this way find that they are no longer jumping from one focus lesson to the next because they have a clear sense of where they're going for the duration of the study. Notice how the issues below closely parallel sections in the unit-of-study overview form.

Issues to consider when planning writing workshop

- Topic/Unit of Study: What the students are studying
- Mini-Lesson Focus: modeling/demonstrating—may focus on qualities of good writing or structures and rituals
- Publication type and date, based on the work students are doing daily leading to publication type and date
- Materials
- Use of Literature/Read Aloud
- Home/School Connection (homework)
- Assessment Tools/Conferring/Ways to Differentiate Instruction
- Reflection

Filling Out Unit-of-Study Overview Forms

How do you decide what to include on the overview forms? It may be helpful to do some thinking on paper first, using the Initial Planning Sheet on the next page. Since one needs to be filled out for each unit, you'll need to make a dozen or so photocopies. The information you fill in will be transferred to the Unit-of-Study Overview Form for each unit. If you are working in a study group, you may find it helpful to complete one or two of these sheets together. Then, do the rest of them on your own or assign them to individual colleagues. At your next meeting, you can share, revise, and edit.

> **To Do:** Make several copies of the Initial Planning Sheet on page 111. Decide how you or your group will complete the work.

Writing Unit of Study
Initial Planning Sheet

Date: _____   Unit of Study: _____

Things to think about when planning the unit of study:

What are the *most important* ideas I want the students to learn about this topic?

_____

_____

_____

_____

How does this fit in with my district's expectations? What expectations will my students be meeting through this unit?

_____

_____

_____

_____

What read alouds would be best for this unit?

_____

_____

_____

_____

What focus lessons are a must?

_____

_____

_____

_____

How long will the unit take?

_____

_____

What type of publishing celebration best fits this type of unit? Have I scheduled a celebration well in advance and let the students and parents know the date?

If so, date of celebration: _____

_____

_____

Take another look at the Yearly Overview Map from Roberts Avenue School on page 97. Then, on this page, see how the teachers there filled out the Initial Planning Sheet for one unit, poetry, and transferred the information to a Unit-of-Study Overview Form.

Writing Unit of Study

Initial Planning Sheet

First Grade, Roberts Avenue School

Date: *Nov./Dec.*   Unit of Study: *Poetry*

Things to think about when planning the unit of study:

What are the *most important* ideas I want the students to learn about this topic?

doesn't have to rhyme   imagery/feeling/mood

close observation to detail   line breaks/white space/form

rhythm/voice/repetition

How does this fit in with my district's expectations? What expectations will my students be meeting through this unit?

first grade curriculum—poetry   sense of self as writer

writing with description   revision/editing skills

What read alouds would be best for this unit?

"April Rain Song" by Langston Hughes

"Things" by Eloise Greenfield

Previous students' work

Poetry that kids bring in and collect from library, mostly non-rhyming

For the Good of the Earth and Sun by Georgia Heard

See attached lists

What focus lessons are a must?

beginning with a feeling

writing about something important   using line breaks and white space

close observation. writing with detail

describing something in a unique way. "beautiful language"

using line breaks and white space

How long will the unit take? *6 weeks*

What type of publishing celebration best fits this type of unit? Have I scheduled a celebration well in advance and let the students and parents know the date?

If so, date of celebration

first poems are type

class anthology

poetry celebration, pa

Writing Unit Overview

Topic/Unit of Study: *Poetry*   **Publication Date:** *12/17*

Type of Publication/Celebration: *poetry recital and individual holiday gifts*

Focus Lessons:

Gathering and immersion	*Line breaks/white space/form*
Close observation/detail	*Awareness of audience*
Poetry doesn't have to rhyme	*Reading aloud/performing*
Rhythm/voice/repetition	*Interpretation*
Imagery/feeling/mood	*Questioning*

Materials:

Transparencies of children's poetry
Georgia Heard's books
A Note Slipped Under the Door by McPhillips and Flynn
Artifacts from nature
Samples of notebook entries reworked as poems

Read Alouds:

All kinds of poetry (mostly un-rhyming).
*   See list in curriculum binder.*
"April Rain Song" by Langston Hughes
"Things" by Eloise Greenfield
Previous students' work

Home/School Connection: (homework)

Bring artifacts from home
Practice reading/reciting poetry
Bring poetry from home

Assessment:

Collect samples of students' work at beginning of unit and at end.
Look for evidence of voice, repetition, beautiful language.

Reflection:

After you have completed a form for each of your units, place it in your binder in the appropriate section. You may want to reorganize or eliminate materials that are currently in your binder, now that you have focused your intentions for study. Start to collect examples of students' work to use at a later date. For example, if a student writes something that sounds like poetry during a revision unit, you can copy it and place it in your binder's poetry section for use later in a focus lesson. Or, if you attend a workshop and get a great list of books for teaching memoir, put it in your binder's memoir section. You can keep blackline masters of record-keeping forms that you have collected or developed. If you find great ideas for focus lessons in professional books or on Web sites, you can add them to the appropriate sections, too.

TEACHER TIP

Carla Monteiro, who teaches at the Tracey School in Norwalk, Connecticut, says this about collecting students' writing to use in focus lessons: "I can't describe how helpful it is to have samples of kids' work in my binder, right where I need them. I make copies and overheads of certain pieces that I know I will need, based on my yearly map. I can use the best samples year after year. It makes planning my daily focus lessons so much easier. I now confer differently, too, always looking for samples of kids' work to use for lessons and knowing where to put them when I find them."

Monthly Planning for Reading

We know that the best reading workshops provide opportunities for whole-group, small- group, and individual instruction delivered through

* Read Aloud,
* Independent Reading,
* Shared Reading,
* Guided Reading.

In reading workshop, what topics do you imagine studying as a whole class? Refer back to the yearly overview map you created in Chapter 4. Then, as you did for writing workshop, fill out the Initial Planning Sheet on the next page for each unit you plan to carry out. From there, transfer the information to the Unit-of-Study Overview Form for reading, which appears on page 109.

Reading Unit of Study
Initial Planning Sheet

Date: _____   Unit of Study: _____

Things to think about when planning the unit of study:

What are the *most important* ideas I want the students to learn about this topic?

_____

_____

_____

_____

How does this fit in with my district's expectations? What expectations will my students be meeting through this unit?

_____

_____

_____

_____

What read alouds would be best for this unit?

_____

_____

_____

_____

What focus lessons are a must?

_____

_____

_____

How long will the unit take? _____

How will we wrap up this unit? What type of reflection will take place? When will the unit end?

_____

_____

_____

Reading Unit Overview

Strategy focus: *Monitoring for Understanding*   **Date:**

Read Aloud: (sample texts)
Stella Luna-Cannon
The Paint Brush Kid-Bulla
My Father's Dragon-Gannett
Book choice models/give book talks

Student Work:
During Read Aloud:
"unfamiliar word/think
detect errors that do not make sense
detect confusing language/concepts
"say something"

During independent reading:
partner monitoring
coding the texts for confusions / unfamiliar words
strategy checklists
oral sampling or punctuation usage
coding the text for discussion spots

Materials:
Post-its
Running record forms
Note-taking forms
A variety of books for book talk and choice
Self-evaluation forms

Focus Lessons:
Using all sources of information
Detecting errors
Problem-solving unknown words
Vocabulary/using context
Stopping when confused/rereading
Phrasing/fluency
Using punctuation to support understanding
Adjusting pace for purpose and difficulty
Inferring author's subtleties in text
Revisiting text to support ideas and understanding
   (literary conversations)
book choic

Shared/Guided Reading (method):
Shared:
cloze procedure using a picture book / shred text
demonstrating chunking
guided book choice (choice within a selected set)

Guided:
word-solving   fluency   rereading

Home/School Connection: (homework)
rereading pages at home
self-evaluation of strategy use

Assessment:
Running records, observ...

Reading Unit Overview

Strategy focus: *Making Connections*   **Date:**

Read Aloud: (sample texts)
Koala Lou-Fox (reminders)
The Pain and the Great One-Blume (T-S)
Oliver Button Is a Sissy-DePaola (T-T)
William's Doll-Zolotow (T-T)
The Keeping Quilt-Polacco (T-W)
Sarah Morton's Day/Samuel Eaton's Day/Tapenum's Day-Waters

Student Work:
During Read Aloud:
"say something" using Post-its in public tries; use journal or response sheet in public tries

During independent reading:
use Post-its to code connections and record a few words, use double-entry journals and quote, picture journal response, response pages (top is Post-it or sketch from text, bottom is explanation of the connection), or story map

Materials:
Journals or appropriate paper: double entry, quote or picture, top/bottom response pages
story map

Focus Lessons:
Think Alouds
Using background knowledge when reading (reminders)
Linking text to own life (text-to-self)
Connecting ideas across the texts (text-to-text)
Linking text to science, social studies understandings
   (text-to-world)
Identifying story elements
Identifying text structures in narrative and expository text
Explaining how the connection helped understanding
Identifying a word or words that support understanding

Shared/Guided Reading (method):
Shared:
Story mapping
Making social studies/science connections

Guided:
Locating connections and explaining understandings

Home/School Connection: (homework)
Rereading of day's pages and completing a Post-it or response entry

Assessment:
Running records, observational notes, Post-its and response entries

---

Here are two examples of Unit-of-Study Overview Forms for second-grade reading workshops, created by teachers in Connecticut's District 6.

Now that you have your monthly plans in place, it's time to start thinking about daily lesson plans. In Chapter 6, we'll consider how to use the monthly plans to create meaningful, organized daily lessons.

Chapter 6

What Do I Do Tomorrow?

*Converting Yearly and Monthly Plans
into Daily Lessons*

"By spending time focusing on our ultimate goals for the students, we've taken the guess-work out of creating daily mini-lessons. We're able to create focus lessons that make sense for the students and feel like they are part of a design, a bigger picture. No more deciding what to do every day on a whim. In the past, the best workshop teachers knew how to do this instinctively. Now we can all create cohesive, meaningful workshops."

—Lynn Holcomb
*Language Arts Coordinator,
Dobbs Ferry, New York*

You've mapped out a year of units for reading and/or writing workshops. You've reflected on the most important aspects of each unit to come up with a monthly focus and plan. So I hope you are beginning to feel a sense of control over your workshop time. Isn't it comforting to know what you will be focusing on and when?

The next step is translating those yearly and monthly plans into daily focus lessons. We'll start by mapping out the weeks, and then get a sense of how each day's focus lesson might go within units. Of course, you won't be able to plan 180 days worth of lessons. That is not the nature of workshop teaching. But, I will share some tips for planning by the week and suggestions for keeping daily lesson plans.

Mapping Out the Weeks

The Weekly Planning Sheet on the next page has proved helpful to many teachers. It is reminiscent of the Yearly Overview Map, but instead of breaking the year down by months, this sheet breaks the month down to weeks.

For each unit of study, certain focus lessons are a must. In fact, you specified many of these lessons in the Unit-of-Study Overview Forms that you filled out in Chapter 5. Look over your lists of focus lessons, unit by unit, and note the ones that make sense at the beginning. Which feel like they belong in the middle of the unit and which would be good at the end? Be sure to leave room for unplanned lessons—ones that need to be taught in response to the work the students are doing. And don't feel compelled to fill in every block. After all, some units will be six weeks long and some as few as two.

As you map out your weekly lesson plans, keep in mind all of the ways to get the information across to students, regardless of your topic. You can:

* model your own reading and writing.

* tell them your point.

* share examples of students' work.

* share examples of published pieces.

Another way to get information across is by asking students to try what you are teaching. For example, to prepare for a focus lesson on stretching out words to get all the sounds down, you can get the ball rolling by

Weekly Planning Sheet

	Monday	Tuesday	Wednesday	Thursday	Friday
Week 1					
Week 2					
Week 3					

118

	Monday	Tuesday	Wednesday	Thursday	Friday
Week 4					
Week 5					
Week 6					

demonstrating this during shared/interactive writing. You can then ask students to come to the chart to share how they would write a particular word. I worked with some kindergarten students recently who showed me how they would write the word *dinosaur*. Their chart looked like this:

```
dnr          ds
xqpj         dnosr
dnsnr
```

From there, I wrote *dinosaur* on the chart and told students that my spelling is the way they would find it in books. (I purposely didn't say the "right" way because I didn't want them to feel like their spelling attempts were wrong.) The point is, it's important to "multiply" your lessons by revisiting a topic often and in a variety of ways. This is the kind of work we should be doing throughout the school year, as we plan.

Remember, no matter what grade you teach, your first unit of study should have something to do with creating a community of readers and/or writers or helping students have a sense of themselves as readers/writers.

As the year goes on, as each unit comes to an end, you'll begin to look toward the next month's focus. Your units may overlap a bit at this stage—and that's okay. Toward the end of a unit on picture books, for example, the students may be spending their time putting finishing touches on their published pieces, while you are trying to get to everyone for an editing conference. During this time, it would make sense for your focus lessons to be related to publishing. At the same time, you can begin immersing the students in the next study—poetry, for example. You can start collecting and reading poetry as a jump start.

In the process, you can fine-tune your poetry unit. Specifically, you can think about what would make sense at the beginning, middle, and end of the unit. You'll also be able to add lessons based on unanticipated needs. Do students still need work with leaving spaces between words? You may not have known this two months ago. That's why it's unwise to plan daily focus lessons too far in advance.

Creating Daily Lesson Plans

It seems every K-2 teacher of reading and writing has a different way of keeping daily lesson plans. When I was teaching first and second grade, I tried several different lesson-plan books and systems before I came up with one that worked for me. I ended up creating my own blank schedule on the computer and printing one out for each day, on a monthly basis. Then, when I did my actual planning, I just filled in the blank spaces. Here's what the morning part of that schedule looked like:

Time	Monday
8:45-9:00 am	Independent Reading Meet With: _____
9:10-9:40 am	Meeting Focus Lesson: (Unit of Study _____) _____ _____ _____
9:45-10:45 am	Reading Workshop Independent Reading Focus: Guided Reading Group: _____ Book Title/Level: _____ Instructional Focus: Guided Reading Group: _____ Book Title/Level: _____ Instructional Focus: Guided Reading Group: _____ Book Title/Level: _____ Instructional Focus:
10:45-11:30 am	Writing Workshop (Unit of Study _____) Focus Lesson: _____ _____ _____ _____
11:30-12:00 pm	Art
12:00-12:35 pm	Lunch

The second-grade teachers at Roberts Avenue School have developed the weekly planning sheet on pages 122 and 123 which they add to their curriculum binders.

Time	Monday	Tuesday	Wednesday
8:30-9:00 am	Independent Reading	Independent Reading	Independent Reading
9:00-9:30 am	Calendar Morning message Poems/Chants Focus Lesson:	Calendar Morning message Poems/Chants Focus Lesson:	Calendar Morning message Poems/Chants Focus Lesson:
9:30-11:00 am	Reading Workshop (HBJ, Guided Reading, Seatwork, Centers) _____ _____ _____ _____ _____	Reading Workshop (HBJ, Guided Reading, Seatwork, Centers) _____ _____ _____ _____ _____	Reading Workshop (HBJ, Guided Reading, Seatwork, Centers) _____ _____ _____ _____ _____
11:00-11:55 am	Writer's Workshop Focus Lesson _____ _____ _____	Writer's Workshop Focus Lesson _____ _____ _____	Writer's Workshop Focus Lesson _____ _____ _____
11:55-12:25 pm	Lunch	Lunch	Lunch
12:25-12:55 pm	Recess	Recess	Recess
12:55-1:10 pm	Read Aloud	Read Aloud	Read Aloud
1:10-1:50 pm	Media	Art	Gym
1:50-2:45 pm	Math obj. _____ _____ _____	Math obj. _____ _____ _____	Math obj. _____ _____ _____
2:45-3:15 pm			

Thursday	Friday	Notes
Independent Reading	Independent Reading	
Calendar Morning message Poems/Chants Focus Lesson:	Calendar Morning message Poems/Chants Focus Lesson:	
Reading Workshop (HBJ, Guided Reading, Seatwork, Centers) _____ _____ _____ _____ _____	Reading Workshop (HBJ, Guided Reading, Seatwork, Centers) _____ _____ _____ _____ _____	
Writer's Workshop Focus Lesson _____ _____ _____	Writer's Workshop Focus Lesson _____ _____ _____	
Lunch	Lunch	
Recess	Recess	
Read Aloud	Read Aloud	
Computers	Music	
Math obj. _____ _____ _____ _____	Math obj. _____ _____ _____ _____	

Mrs. Masi
First Grade Afternoon Lesson Plan
Day: _____   Date: _____

11:15 am	Prepare for Lunch
11:20-11:50 am	Lunch
11:50-12:20 pm	Recess
12:25-12:40 pm	Read Aloud
12:45-1:30 pm	Writing Workshop Mini-Lesson Topic: _____ Materials Needed:
1:30-1:45 pm	Writing Share Focus:
1:55-2:30 pm	Specials
2:40-3:20 pm	Math

Michele Masi, first-grade teacher at Roberts Avenue School, keeps her lesson plans similar to the way I did. She types up a form and fills in details on a day-to-day basis.

This last example shows one teacher's daily lesson plan for beginning a unit of study on Making Connections to Text in reading.

Deciding what to teach on a daily basis becomes so much easier when you have monthly plans in place. Try some of the ideas in this chapter, modifying them as you see fit. Then share your plans with colleagues. There are many resources containing sample focus lessons. Refer to pages 67 and 68 for some helpful titles.

Making Connections to Text
Sample Focus Lessons, Denise Bozutto, CT Regional District 6

Focus Lesson: Making Connections—reminders
(using background knowledge when reading)

Read Aloud: *Koala Lou*
Teacher uses think-aloud about connection she/he is making that reminds her/him of something. On a Post-it marked "R," teacher writes a few words about the connection to mark the spot in the text. (Post-it sticks out of book.)

Student Work:

During Read Aloud—During the last few pages of the text, students "say something" to their Read Aloud partner that reminds them of something. Teacher records on chart connection categories: text to self, text to text, text to world. Teacher may also have students do a 'public try' of the strategy in the rug area (i.e each student reads for 3 minutes and recording a Post-it).

During independent reading—Students use three to four Post-its to record a few words to describe connections. During last five minutes of independent reading, students pair-share with a partner, discussing their Post-its.

During share—Teacher fishbowls a partnership with model responses or selects two or three students to share a Post-it. Teacher reviews objective: "Why is it important to think about what the text reminds you of?" and "Why is it important for your reading?"

Homework: Students reread today's pages and complete one more

---

Focus Lesson: Making Connections—reminders
(written response to text)

Read Aloud: *The Relatives Came* by Cynthia Rylant
On large chart paper, teacher models using a double-entry journal, using yesterday's Post-its. Teacher thinks aloud the process.

Student Work:

During Read Aloud—Students "say something" to their Read Aloud partner that could be written for last few Post-its. Teacher records responses.

During Independent Read—Students continue coding their text with R and a few words. During last ten minutes of independent reading, students record in double-entry journals and share with a partner.

During share—Two to three students share model entries. Teacher reviews why it is important to make text-to-self connections when reading.

Homework: Reread pages you have read today and complete another double-entry journal entry.

7

Reflections

"*I'm still learning.*"
—Michelangelo,
at the end
of his life

During one of our last meetings of the school year, Kathy, Kay, and Michele from Roberts Avenue School and I reflected on the process of planning for the year. They had just finished their second year of teaching using units of study and curriculum binders. All three teachers agreed that they had never seen students grow so much in a single year. Kay attributed it to the fact that they got started right away with assessments. They didn't wait until the end of September. Planning and using the curriculum binder also helped them get their workshops up and running right away. For the first time, they started writing workshop and independent reading on the first day of school. By the end of September, they were amazed at how smoothly everything was running.

Having a yearly plan helped them make sense of workshop teaching. A big relief for them was feeling like they didn't have to follow the teacher's manuals, page by page. They felt empowered to make the right decisions for the students in their rooms. According to Kathy, "I no longer feel the pressure of wondering what I am going to do next." The children are central to her daily lesson planning because she has the framework of the units of study to keep her organized. Her focus has shifted.

At the end of each unit of study, they spent some time reflecting and making notes on their monthly planning sheets. What went really well during the unit? What will we do differently next time? They'll find that they will refer back to these notes while planning in the future.

The second-grade teachers were equally impressed with the students' literacy development. Their students, who had been in Kathy, Michelle, and Kay's rooms the year before, came to school with excellent literacy skills. The teachers commented that they had never seen second graders come with so much confidence and such high reading levels. The first-grade teachers feel strongly that intentional teaching was the reason.

At the end-of-year meeting, the teachers did decide to change a few things in their yearly plan. For example, they moved the poetry unit to a different month. And it was easy—they just opened the three-ring binder, took out the relevant material, and shifted it. They also planned some summer reading of professional books. All in all, they became used to the idea of thinking of themselves as researchers of teaching.

Planning for successful reading and writing is not something that you ever really finish. It is a work in progress, in need of constant refinement, as it should be. As you gain more knowledge by reading research-based materials, attending staff development programs, and learning with your students, you will add new information to your binders and curriculum plans. If this book has done nothing more than encourage you to view yourself as a researcher of teaching, then I've met my goal.

> "I never thought about these things when I considered planning before, my schedule, the room arrangement, materials . . . . I feel so in control now, like my teaching makes sense."
>
> —Kathy Hamilton, second-grade teacher, Roberts Avenue School

Bibliography

Calkins, Lucy McCormick. *The Art of Teaching Reading*. New York: Addison Wesley, 2001.

—*The Art of Teaching Writing*. Portsmouth, NH: Heinemann, 1994.

Clay, Marie M. *An Observation Survey of Early Literacy Achievement*. Portsmouth, NH: Heinemann, 1993.

Fairfax County Schools, Department of Instructional Services. *Primary Purposes: Getting Started*. Fairfax County, VA.

Fountas, Irene C., and Gay Su Pinnell. *Guided Reading: Good First Teaching for All Children*. Portsmouth, NH: Heinemann, 1996.

—*Guiding Readers and Writers, 3-6: Teaching Comprehension, Genre, and Content Literacy*. Portsmouth, NH: Heinemann, 2001.

Harvey, Stephanie, and Anne Goudvis. *Strategies That Work: Teaching Comprehension to Enhance Understanding*. York, ME: Stenhouse, 2000.

Gentry, J. Richard. *The Literacy Map: Guiding Children to Where They Need to Be (K-3)*. New York: Mondo Publishing, 2000.

Hindley, Joanne. *In the Company of Children*. Portland, ME: Stenhouse, 1996.

Keene, Ellin Oliver, and Susan Zimmerman. *Mosaic of Thought: Teaching Comprehension in a Reader's Workshop*. Portsmouth, NH: Heinemann, 1997.

Nia, Isoke Titilayo. "Units of Study in the Writing Workshop." *Primary Voices K-6*, v.8, no.1, NCTE, 1999.

Ray, Katie Wood, with Lester Laminack. *The Writing Workshop: Working Through the Hard Parts (And They're All Hard Parts)*. Urbana, Il: National

Council of Teachers of English, 2001.

Schulman, Mary Browning, and Carleen DaCruz Payne. *Guided Reading: Making It Work*. New York: Scholastic, 2000.

Taberski, Sharon. *On Solid Ground: Strategies for Teaching Reading, K–3*. Portsmouth, NH: Heinemann, 2000.

The University of Pittsburgh and the National Center on Education and the Economy. *Reading and Writing Grade by Grade: Primary Literacy Standards for Kindergarten Through Third Grade*, 1999.

Weaver, Constance, Lorraine Gillmeister-Krause, and Grace Vento-Zogby. *Creating Support for Effective Literacy Education*. Portsmouth, NH: Heinemann, 1996.

Wrubel, Ronit. *Great Group Strategies: Dozens of Ways to Flexibly Group Your Students for Maximum Learning Across the Curriculum*. New York: Scholastic, 2002.